Eat WELL Feel GOOD

PRACTICAL PALEO LIVING

Over 200 Recipes
of Paleo-Inspired Dishes

by Diane Frampton

Eat WELL Feel GOOD
www.practicalpaleoliving.com

Copyright © 2011 Diane Frampton
All Rights Reserved.

Printed in the United States of America

Editorial Consultants: Sarah Belk and Christine Barrett
Nutritional Consultant: Diana Rodgers, NTP
Art Director: Kristen Villalongo
Illustratons by Katelyn Marcotte
Photos: Veer.com

ISBN 978-0-578-08342-1

Eat WELL Feel GOOD

Eat WELL Feel GOOD is a compilation of healthy recipes that follow the simple premise of eating real foods. This is not a traditional cookbook. You won't find flour, sugar, grains or dairy in any of the recipes. Why? Because the book follows the theory of Paleo eating to support good overall health with the focus of improved digestion and balanced insulin levels.

The recipes were inspired primarily from eating a Paleo diet and while you may find an ingredient or two, like wine and vinegar, which cause you to say "that's not Paleo!", relax. These recipes are designed to taste great while helping you stick to a Paleo lifestyle.

Expand your comfort zone in the kitchen; you'll probably be surprised at all the easy cooking methods and mouth-watering flavor combinations in this book.

My personal theory: don't take cooking so seriously! Approach each recipe as a "starting place" then add, omit, adjust, change, tweak and create the meal you want! That's what makes cooking fun.

As you enjoy the recipes in *Eat WELL Feel GOOD* you'll realize how great Paleo-style food tastes. But most of all, you'll discover that eating well makes you feel wonderful!

Acknowledgements

First of all, this cookbook wouldn't exist without the encouragement of my fellow CrossFit friends and without my sister, Nichole, who dragged me to my first CrossFit class four years ago. Thank you.

Many thanks to my friend Suzanne, without whose initial typing assistance, this book couldn't have happened.

Thanks to my nutritional consultant Diana Rodgers for her wisdom, expertise and humor.

My gratitude to the team that helped me put it all together. To my editorial consultants, Sarah Belk, for helping me start this project and her unwavering support and Christine Barrett, for jumping into this project with great tenacity to help me finish it! I thank you for your kindness and patience. To my designers, Katie Marcotte and Kristen Villalongo, who took my words and brought them to life with such visual clarity. You are both amazing. Your tireless efforts, talents and patience will not be forgotten. Thanks to Cam Brown for introducing me to the aforementioned team and believing that his friend could actually pull this off.

Lastly, special love and thanks to my husband, Kurt and our daughters, Kim and Kate for believing, supporting and tolerating me throughout this entire process. I love you.

Contents

My STORY

Food, weight, nutrition and digestion have been issues for me for nearly my entire life. By the age of 18, I'd already met with numerous doctors and nutritionists and knew what Metamucil, Alka-Seltzer, Pepto-Bismol and Zantac were. In all the years of struggling with my diet, weight and health, I didn't consider how it was impacting my *overall* health.

I struggled with my weight and digestive issues through adolescence and into adulthood. I had an unhealthy relationship with food even though I loved to cook. As a result, I became resentful about how food made me feel.

I spent many of my adult years, particularly after I had children, trying to lose weight and regain my health. I tried so many diets! Some worked (i.e., I lost weight), but I always felt deprived. Most diets left me feeling hungry, but I continued to exert enough will power to follow the diet. I now realize one of the problems with those diets was the focus on calorie restriction; I concentrated on consuming minimal calories to keep from gaining weight. I could tolerate the low calorie diets for short periods of time but hunger and deprivation would soon take over and the vicious cycle would begin. I'd indulge in what I considered to be a well-deserved binge. The binging led to weeks of high calorie and processed food consumption to satisfy my cravings. Every time this happened, the weight I'd lost would come back; usually with a little extra. I yo-yoed like this for years and always exercised just enough to convince myself I was healthy.

Four years ago, I met Dave Picardy, trainer and owner of North Shore CrossFit and my life began to change. I was introduced to the fitness and nutritional philosophy called CrossFit.

Greg Glassman, founder of CrossFit, advises that we "eat meat and vegetables, nuts and seeds, some fruit, little starch and no sugar. Keep intake to levels that will support exercise but not body fat. Practice and train major lifts: deadlift, clean, squat, presses, clean and jerk, and snatch. Similarly, master the basics of gymnastics: pull-ups, dips, rope climb, push-ups, sit-ups, presses to handstand, pirouettes, flips, splits and holds. Bike, run, swim, row, etc., hard and fast. Five or six days per week mix these elements in as many combinations and patterns as creativity will allow. Routine is the enemy. Keep workouts short and intense. Regularly learn and play new sports."

CrossFit has been called "The Sport of Fitness" because CrossFit reintroduces personal athletic achievement and performance to training. The mindset at the start of each workout is to be stronger, move faster and more efficiently with better form than ever. For more information about CrossFit, check out www.crossfit.com.

I love CrossFit because the workouts are demanding, fun, challenging and help push me to be my absolute best. The community of fellow CrossFitters is amazing and a fundamental part of the overall program.

While learning how to be a CrossFitter, the nutritional component of CrossFit was prescribed, often discussed and encouraged through workshops and seminars, plus one-on-one support offered at the gym. I stubbornly ignored this nutritional component because I had convinced myself if I worked out hard enough, my weight issues would be corrected. I was making considerable progress with my fitness goals; I became much stronger and was proud of it. However, I was so focused on my physical goals as a CrossFitter that I let my digestion problems take a back seat. I ignored the stomach aches, heartburn and constipation. I knew that in order to address these issues, I was probably going to have to give up my addiction to carbohydrates and sugar, which were clearly unfolding as one of the major contributors to my weight problems.

My frustration began to build when I started to hit a plateau with my fitness goals. The food I was feeding my body and the responses my body was having were impacting my energy levels, recovery time, and limiting my overall strength. I began to seriously look at my food choices to help me address my health because I believed they were having a significant impact on my performance and I wasn't really feeling good.

I decided to commit to the 30-Day Paleo Challenge: no dairy, no grains, no sugar, no alcohol. For thirty days! I did it and I've never looked back. I'll admit that the first two weeks were quite difficult. I experienced a loss of energy and sugar cravings that nearly drove me crazy! However, I stuck with it and worked hard to stay focused. I found it helpful to reassure myself that I could do anything for 30 days. I can't even explain how I felt by week three. I couldn't believe that it was even possible to feel this good; seriously! By the end of the third week, I knew this was a life-changing experience. I continue to live a Paleo lifestyle by making good Paleo food choices, moving my body every day and getting 7–8 hours of sleep. I eat Paleo about 95% of the time and I no longer struggle with weight or digestion issues. I have lost over 40 pounds, have regulated my digestion, my skin glows, I have great energy and increased strength. I feel better and I look better.

Although I follow a Paleo lifestyle, I am not an expert on the science of Paleo nutrition. But I am a firm believer of the nutritional science that supports this type of eating and lifestyle. I work every day to educate myself and others in hopes of encouraging those who want to improve their lives.

It is not my intention to present you with the "everything you need to know about Paleo guide," but merely to share with you my own personal experiences, research, and observations of others. At the end of this book, I've included a list of resources for more information about the Paleo lifestyle.

I started this journey trying to put together a couple of recipes for friends. The more recipes I put together, the more people asked for them; they told their friends and the next thing I knew, my recipes spiraled into a cookbook project which became *Eat WELL Feel GOOD, Practical Paleo Living*. As you read through the recipes, keep in mind the writer is a working mom, not a professional chef, whose goal is to make healthy dishes for herself and her family.

For more information, follow me and my Paleo/CrossFit lifestyle at www.practicialpaleoliving.com.

Introduction
by Diana Rodgers, NTP

"99.9% of our genes were formed before the development of agriculture"
—Dr. S. Boyd Eaton, MD, Medical Anthropologist

What is Paleo?

Paleo is short for Paleolithic, the time period 10,000 years ago. The premise of a Paleo diet centers around the idea that our bodies have not adapted sufficiently to eating foods that weren't available to us during that time. It is thought that more than 70% of food consumed today was never available in Paleolithic times and therefore isn't digested effectively. We put so much processed food into our bodies, most of which makes us unhealthy. The advances in agriculture and mass food production have caused us to move away from eating real food; food meant to work *with* our bodies for optimal health.

A Paleo diet involves eating meat and vegetables, nuts and seeds, little starch, some fruit and no sugar. It means no grains, legumes, dairy or alcohol. It means staying away from all processed foods. It means eating as our hunter-gather ancestors did. The Standard American Diet (SAD) is riddled with refined sugars, adulterated vegetable oils, dairy products and grains, all of which can lead to obesity, heart disease and type-2 diabetes. Diet-related chronic diseases represent the largest cause of death in America. These diseases were rare or nonexistent in the Paleolithic Era and can largely be blamed on excessive consumption of modern foods including grains, refined sugars, processed vegetable oils and industrially-raised meats.

Why are grains forbidden?

Grains can irritate the gut and can lead to hypoglycemia. Grains and legumes contain a variety of anti-nutritional components such as lectins,

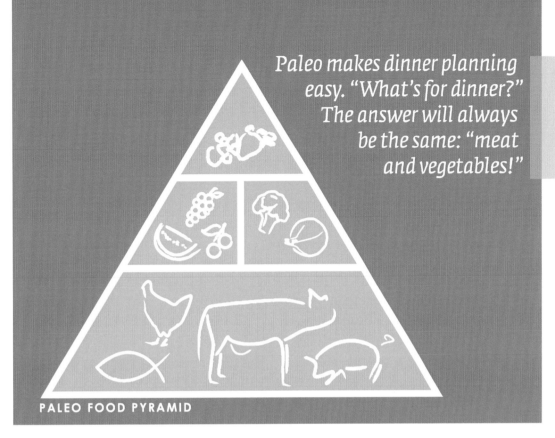

Paleo makes dinner planning easy. "What's for dinner?" The answer will always be the same: "meat and vegetables!"

PALEO FOOD PYRAMID

saponins, and phytic acid. Lectins (sugar-binding proteins) can irritate the lining of the gastrointestinal tract which interferes with digestion, nutrient absorption and stimulates shifts in bacterial flora. Lectins are particularly damaging in the form of gluten-containing grains such as wheat (including wheat germ), rye and barley. Lectins are not broken down in the normal digestive process thus leaving large, intact proteins in the gut. When these large protein molecules enter our bloodstream, they are easily mistaken for foreign invaders like bacteria, viruses or parasites. When this happens, the immune system mounts an attack on those foreign proteins and makes antibodies against them. Saponins impair the digestion of protein and the uptake of vitamins and minerals in the gut, and may cause hypoglycemia. Phytic acid has been proven to inhibit absorption of minerals and trace elements such as iron, zinc, calcium, magnesium and manganese. The moral of the story? If you're looking to restore digestive health and regulate your blood sugar, cut out all grains and legumes.

What about dairy?

There is plenty of good research indicating that milk consumption is not optimal. Milk has some good qualities; some people manage milk consumption just fine. But most do not because it's high in lactose. Lactose digestion is difficult for many, and some are allergic to casein, the protein in milk.

What about fat?

Fat is a much more powerful fuel for our bodies than sugar and starch. "The human body and brain's primary source of fuel is designed to be fat in the form of ketones—not glucose," says Nora Gedgaudas in her book, *Primal Body, Primal Mind*. Ketosis occurs when the body is burning fat, not glucose, as its primary fuel. Picture fat as the slow-burning log on the fire and sugar is like paper, which burns very quickly. Basically you can get enough of what your body needs from a Paleo diet to thrive just as our ancestors did before bread, bagels, pasta and cake became part of today's diet.

What about canola oil and other fats?

Canola, soy, corn and other vegetable oils are highly-processed and were not available to our Paleolithic ancestors. These monounsaturated oils are very heat sensitive and the high heat they are exposed to during the extraction process renders them toxic to the body. This leads to free-radical formation and can cause inflammation. A diet high in these oils can damage our cell membranes which need saturated fats.

In addition, when we eat healthy fats, our gallbladders send a message to our brains telling us that we're full. People who eat low-fat foods high in vegetable oils (instead of natural, saturated fats like butter and coconut oil), don't receive the critical message from the brain, "I'm full," so they tend to overeat. Most fats consumed by people today come from these unhealthy oils, trans-fats and from omega-6 fats.

"In a Framingham, Massachusetts study, the more saturated fat one ate, the more cholesterol one ate, the more calories one ate, the lower people's serum cholesterol. We found that people who ate the most cholesterol, ate the most saturated fat, ate the most calories weighed the least and were the most physically active."

—*Archives of Internal Medicine*, 1992. Dr. William Castilli, Director of the Framingham Study.

Numerous studies have concluded the following results for those on a Paleo diet:
- Weight loss
- Improved glucose tolerance

- Lowered blood pressure
- Significant reductions in total cholesterol, low-density lipoproteins (LDL) and triglycerides
- Increased feeling of satiation

Eating a Paleo diet isn't just for weight loss. According to the *European Journal of Clinical Nutrition Advance Online Publication*, "Even short-term consumption of a Paleolithic type diet improves blood pressure and glucose tolerance, decreases insulin secretion, increases insulin sensitivity and improves lipid profiles without weight loss in healthy humans."

The Paleo diet is not just another diet. It is a lifestyle; a change in the way you eat and live. It's a journey to find the foods that make you healthy and feel good. Listen to your body after you have had a snack, meal or drink and honestly ask yourself if you feel good. Most importantly, determine how good you feel hours later or the following day.

Do I need to eat strictly Paleo forever?

For some people, keeping a 95%–100% Paleo diet is the only way to stay healthy. For others, 85% adherence to the Paleo principals is good enough. I strongly suggest a strict 30-Day Paleo Challenge at some point to reset your body's insulin response to foods and to heal your stomach from damage due to the Standard American Diet.

In conclusion, eating like our hunter-gather ancestors may not be the answer to all your health and diet concerns. If you find that your cravings are still out of control or your weight is still not where you want it to be, consider visiting a Paleo nutritionist for some advice about diet-tweaking and digestive supplements. I highly recommend reading *The Paleo Solution*, by Robb Wolf to learn more about the science and success of living Paleo.

Eating Paleo may be easier than you think and this cookbook is a great way for someone to start. Read the science, but try the recipes and see how good you feel.

Following a PALEO Diet/Lifestyle: Getting Started

If you've thought about trying to eat Paleo but don't know how to begin, here are a few ideas to help you get started; try not to overthink it.

Clean out your pantry and refrigerator.
Remove ALL non-Paleo foods like pasta, rice, crackers, cereal, flour, sugar, milk, juices, dressings, and jams! Give these foods to non-Paleo friends or, if unopened, to your local food bank. It's best not to have tempting food in the house, especially when you first begin.

Exception.
If you feel you must keep some non-Paleo foods and snacks in your house (like I do) for the kids, designate one small cupboard area and limit the number of offerings. The better you eat, the better your kids will eat. My kids eat all-Paleo dinners and for the most part, breakfast as well. Lunch is still a work in progress.

Go Shopping.
Fill your kitchen with good Paleo food choices. Having the right foods on hand make healthy cooking and snacking easier. Use the Paleo Food List (pages 14–15) for inspiration. For beginners, here's a short, simple list to help get you started.

Proteins: beef, poultry, pork, shrimp, fish

Vegetables: all, except for corn and peas

Fruits: choose berries, oranges, apples and pears to start

Fats: coconut oil, ghee (recipe, page 63), olive oil, avocados

Herbs and Spices: as many as you can find

Flours: almond and coconut

Beverages: water, coconut water, seltzer water, herbal tea

Okay, LET'S DO IT!

Eat protein, fat and vegetables at every meal.
Eat until you are satisfied, but don't stuff yourself. Eat when you are hungry, but you probably won't be hungry during this adjustment. If you are, add a little more protein and fat to your meals.

Get comfortable eating fat!**
Good fats are good for you. They will help you feel full and they work to fuel your body.

Limit fruit to once a day if weight loss is a goal.
Eat foods that satisfy your hunger, but remember that fruit can spike your insulin levels. The goal is to maintain an even level of blood sugar throughout the day. No spikes.

Limit nuts as a snack if weight loss is a goal.
However, if you love nuts use them to replace other fats (like ghee and coconut oil) at mealtime.

Drink and sleep.
Drink plenty of water. You may also have herbal tea and mineral water. Rest is important, too: try to get at least 7 to 8 hours of sleep every night.

Move your body every day.
If you rarely exercise, start with walking. If you already workout regularly, keep it up!

**Know Your Fats!
Fats to eat: *Saturated fats:* coconut oil, ghee, (clarified butter; see recipe, page 63), lard, chicken or duck fat, butter*, fat from grass-fed beef.

*The use of butter should be avoided during the first 30 days of a strict Paleo diet plan.
Unsaturated fats: olive oil, sesame oil, nut oils, flaxseed oil, avocados, nuts, seeds

Fats to avoid: *Saturated:* margarine, hydrogenated oils, partially hydrogenated oils, trans-fats, fat from meat that is commercially raised.
Unsaturated: canola oil, corn oil, vegetable oil, soybean oil, grapeseed oil

Let's COOK!

Start Cooking.

Get creative in the kitchen and start making meals with good, wholesome Paleo-friendly food.

Chop, slice, dice and get the whole family to help with meal preparations. When kids get involved in cooking, they're proud of the end result; the meal is "theirs" and they'll be more likely to eat and enjoy it.

The Paleo Meal.

Robb Wolf, author of *The Paleo Solution*, came up with the Paleo Food Matrix which reduces meal preparation to the basics!

Example: Pick a protein, a fat, a vegetable, and some spices.
(Use the food list, pages 14–15, as your guide.)

1 Put some fat in a pan
2 Brown the protein
3 Add herbs and spices
4 Add vegetables
5 EAT

You can take it a step further and add extra flavor with salsa, tomato paste, lemon or lime juice or vinegars.

Use the food lists (pages 14–15) in this book to begin a Paleo-eating program or make a list of your own Paleo-friendly favorites.

The Paleo CHALLENGE

If you decide to take the 30-Day Paleo Challenge, remember that the first few weeks may be difficult; you might initially feel tired and shaky as a result of the body's adjustment to its insulin levels. Make sure to seek out support and know that your body should adjust by week three, if not sooner.

Keep in mind that you will be able to incorporate a few things back into your diet after the strict 30 days. You may find that you can have more fruit, or incorporate some natural sugar sources, like honey.

Think of it this way: the worst case scenario is that you spent a month without some of the foods you really like. The best case scenario is that you discover you're able to live healthier and feel better then you ever expected.

A Paleo lifestyle is not a one-size-fits-all approach. Everyone's body is different and our responses to dietary changes will vary. Listen to your body and start to get in touch with how food consumption makes you feel. Remember your personal nutritional and fitness needs and goals. As with any diet or lifestyle change, make sure to consult your physician, particularly if you have any significant health issues.

My Paleo FOOD LIST

Fats

Coconut Milk Ghee
Almond Milk Lard
Coconut Oil Bacon Fat
Olive Oil
Sesame Oil

Proteins

Eggs Lamb
Chicken Tilapia
Turkey Salmon
Duck Tuna
Pork Sardines
Sausage Shrimp
Bacon Lobster
Beef Scallops
Veal Clams
Bison Oysters

Nuts & Seeds

Walnuts
Almonds
Cashews
Macadamia Nuts
Pecans
Pine Nuts
Pistachios
Hazelnuts
Brazil Nuts
Pumpkin Seeds
Sunflower Seeds
Sesame Seeds

Fruits

Melons Kiwi
Blueberries Papayas
Blackberries Mangoes
Strawberries Coconut
Raspberries Bananas
Cranberries Pineapple
Cherries Apricots
Lemons Peaches
Limes Nectarines
Oranges Figs
Pomegranates Plums
Unsweetened Avocados
   Frozen Fruit Tomatoes
Apples
Pears
Grapefruit
Rhubarb
Grapes

Vegetables

Onions
Garlic
Shallots
Plantains
Sweet Potatoes
Butternut Squash
Acorn Squash
Spaghetti Squash
Delicata Squash
Pumpkin (fresh or canned)
Arugula
Spinach
Mixed Greens
Kale
Bok Choy
Lettuce (all types)
Cabbage (red, green, napa)
Celery
Zucchini/Summer Squash

Chard
Asparagus
Artichokes
Peppers (all kinds)
Beets
Radishes
Parsnips
Carrots
Turnips
Broccoli
Cauliflower
Daikon
Jicama
Leeks
Cucumbers
Mushrooms
Fennel
Eggplant
Scallions

Condiments, Spices and More

Dijon Mustard
Tomato Paste
Canned Tomatoes
Capers
Horseradish
Canned Chipotles
  in Adobo Sauce
Broths (chicken,
  beef, vegetable)
Tahini
SunButter
Almond Butter
Cashew Butter
Balsamic Vinegar
Red Wine Vinegar

Unfiltered Apple Cider
  Vinegar
Tamari
  (wheat-free soy sauce)
Cinnamon
Cumin
Allspice
Coriander
Ginger (fresh or ground)
Garlic (fresh or powder)
Cayenne Pepper
Cardamom
Chili Powder
Paprika
Red Pepper Flakes

Turmeric
Emeril's Essence
  Seasoning
Cilantro
Basil
Oregano
Rosemary
Thyme
Marjoram
Dill
Sea Salt
Black Pepper
Almond Flour
Raw Honey
Sage

BEYOND *the Paleo Food List*

Sweeteners: These aren't all Paleo, but they make great dessert treats and keep me happy: apricots, cherries, raisins, prunes, Medijool dates, maple syrup, raw honey, coconut crystals, coconut nectar, unsweetened applesauce and bananas.

Herbs: Although the list of ingredients for most recipes indicates dried herbs, use fresh whenever possible. Many of these recipes call for dried to make the recipes easy for the novice cook. Buying, growing, and using fresh herbs will make a significant difference in the flavor of the finished dish. Note: roughly 1 teaspoon of dried equals 1 tablespoon of fresh.

Although it's easy to find Paleo-friendly foods (especially meat and vegetables) at the supermarket, some Paleo ingredients may require shopping at a specialty-food store or online.

Almond Flour: Although most large grocery stores now carry this in the organic section, I sometimes order it online because the quality of the flour is better for baking (finer grind) at www.benefityourlifestore.com, www.digestivewellness.com or www.barryfarms.com.

Chocolate: I like to use Dagoba chocolate products. You can find them at Whole Foods or online at www.dagoba.com, www.benefityourlife.com, or www.worldpantry.com.

Sweeteners: Raw honey, coconut nectar, coconut crystals and agave can be found in the organic section of large grocery stores; Whole Foods carries all of them.

Coconut Flour, Coconut Butter, Coconut Oil: Whole Foods sells all of these but many large grocery stores carry them in the organic section as well.

Flaxseed Flour: Look for this in the organic section of large grocery stores.

Substitutions

Eating well is easier than you think. Many of my old recipes became Paleo-friendly with just a few changes. Mostly, I just removed the grains, but below are a few suggestions for reinventing some of your own favorite recipes.

If recipe calls for:	Try this:
Sugar or brown sugar	Coconut Crystals, Date Paste (dates mashed with a little warm water)
Agave	Coconut Nectar, Unsweetened Applesauce, Molasses, Maple Syrup, Date Paste, Raw Honey
Flour	Almond Flour or Coconut Flour (use the same amount of almond meal as regular flour. However, coconut flour is very dense; use about ¼ cup coconut flour for each cup of regular flour)
Butter	Ghee (page 63) or Coconut Oil
Canola Oil	Coconut Oil
Chocolate	Unsweetened or no less than 73% Cacoa
Bread Crumbs	Almond, Walnut or Pecan Meal
Rice or Grains	Cauliflower "Rice" (page 113) or any Vegetable
Potatoes	Sweet Potatoes
Milk	Coconut Milk or Almond Milk
Peanut Butter	Almond, Cashew or SunButter

SNACK *Ideas*

- Nuts: a handful or two (less, if weight loss is your goal)

- Pumpkin or sunflower seeds: a handful or two

- A piece or portion of fruit: an apple, an orange or a cup of berries (have a handful of nuts, too, if you're really hungry)

- Pieces of cooked chicken breasts (leftovers or freshly cooked)

- Slices of avocados wrapped in turkey or ham slices. (Avoid the deli; look for organic turkey and ham.) Make sure to purchase meats that are the least processed and nitrate-free such as Applegate Farms. Good options are available at Whole Foods and Trader Joe's.

- Beef jerky (homemade or store-bought)

- Couple of handfuls of chopped or baby carrots, red bell peppers or cucumber slices

- Carrots or celery dipped into SunButter, almond butter or cashew butter

- Any leftover vegetables or meats

- Lettuce "boats" filled with any leftover meats or vegetables

- Egg Muffin (recipe, page 28)

- Small Apple Muffin (recipe, page 30) or Banana Nut Muffin (recipe, page 41) (try to eat muffins with protein if possible)

- Roasted beets (I love chunks of warm or chilled roasted beets!)

- Prosciutto-wrapped asparagus

- Slice of sweet potato or Banana Bread (recipe, page 213) with nut butter (good before a workout)

- Hard boiled eggs

- Beet Hummus (recipe, page 67) with carrots and celery

Clean out your pantry. Get rid of grains, cereals and non-Paleo snacks.

Planning is Important:
BE PREPARED

Prep
Make sure you take the time to prepare for the week ahead. I usually prep meals on Sunday which makes weekday meals quick and easy.

Chop
Chop onions, peppers and other vegetables you will need for the week. I always chop extra onion and peppers for last minute breakfast ideas.

Snack
Have your favorite vegetables—carrots, celery, peppers, etc.—cut up and ready for fast snacks. Or keep a roasted chicken in the refrigerator for easy protein "picking." Remember, the goal is to keep good Paleo food choices on hand.

Store
Hardy vegetables like sweet potatoes and butternut squash can be peeled and chopped then stored in the refrigerator for up to a week before using.

Cook
Make a lot. Whatever you're cooking, make a big batch. Save (or freeze) some for a future breakfast, lunch or even another dinner.

Freeze
Many recipes can be easily frozen. Place leftovers in lunch-sized containers and freeze for an easy lunch-on-the-go or for a quick supper.

Beverages

The Paleo diet in its most restricted sense advises that you only drink water. This is not a realistic goal for most people; however, it is important to drink plenty of water throughout the day, everyday!

Here are some other Paleo-friendly choices: unsweetened herbal tea (hot or cold), plain or flavored (unsweetened) seltzer water, club soda, unsweetened cranberry juice or coconut water.

While drinking alcohol is not recommended as part of the Paleo lifestyle, it is unrealistic to think many of us are not going to indulge once in a while. So, when you do, try one of the Paleo-friendly drink ideas in this chapter.

Robb Wolf's Margarita

2   shots (2 ounces) of tequila over ice

Juice from 1 whole lime

Splash of soda water

Vodka and Soda

1   shot (one ounce) vodka

Lemon or lime juice, to taste

1   cup soda water

Vodka (or liquor of choice) and Cranberry Juice

1   shot (one ounce) vodka over ice

1   shot (one ounce) unsweetened cranberry juice

1   cup soda water

(Note: If the unsweetened cranberry juice is too tart for you, add a teaspoon of honey.)

Vodka Lemonade

1   shot (one ounce) vodka over ice
Lemon juice, to taste
1   cup water
1-2 teaspoons raw honey

Vodka Lemonade & Cucumber Juice

Add the juice of one small, peeled cucumber to Vodka Lemonade.

Red Wine

Enjoy a glass!

Remember, alcohol can disturb your sleep—a vital part of good health—so try to have that drink early in the evening so your body has time to process it.

Breakfast

What's better than bacon and eggs? For Paleo enthusiasts, breakfast can be the easiest meal of the day. Eggs are so versatile; I enjoy them at least five days a week. When I crave an egg-less breakfast, there are plenty of options. And remember: tonight's dinner can often become tomorrow's breakfast!

Breakfast Smoothie

1   cup coconut milk

1   cup frozen or fresh mixed berries

1   tablespoon vanilla extract

2   tablespoons of any nut butter (optional)

Water

Mix all ingredients except water in blender and blend until smooth. Add water as needed for desired consistency. Makes 2 servings.

Kurt's Morning Smoothie

2   scoops vegan protein powder, such as Sun Warrior

Small handful of almonds

1   handful spinach

1   cup frozen mixed berries

1   banana

2   cups water

Blend all ingredients in a blender until smooth. Makes 2 servings.

Breakfast Squares

1½ cups almond flour
¼   teaspoon sea salt
¼   teaspoon baking soda
¼   cup coconut oil, melted
¼   cup raw honey
2   teaspoons vanilla extract
½   cup shredded unsweetened coconut
½   cup pumpkin seeds
½   cup sunflower seeds
½   cup slivered almonds
¼   cup raisins or currants

These Breakfast Squares are terrific for snacks, too!

Preheat oven to 350 degrees F.

In a small bowl combine almond flour, salt and baking soda; set aside.

In a large bowl combine coconut oil, honey and vanilla; mix well.

Stir dry mixture into wet mixture.

Mix in coconut, pumpkin seeds, sunflower seeds, slivered almonds and raisins and mix well.

Grease an 8×8 baking dish with coconut oil. Press the dough into the baking dish; wet your hands with water to help pat the dough down evenly. Bake for 20–25 minutes. Cool for 5 minutes, then cut into squares. Makes 16 squares.

Add ½ cup chocolate chips and Breakfast Squares become Dessert Squares!

Crumbled leftover Breakfast Squares can be used to top Apple Pie (recipe, page 224) or Fruit Cobbler (recipe, page 220). So good!

Egg Muffins

These muffins are famous treats in the Paleo world and recipes for them can be found on almost any Paleo site, but here's how we like them:

1   tablespoon olive oil

1   sweet onion, chopped

1   sweet red pepper, chopped

½   pound of ground turkey or pork sausage

1   teaspoon cayenne pepper

12   eggs

½   teaspoon each sea salt and pepper

1   cup of spinach, chopped

Preheat oven to 350 degrees F.

Heat olive oil in a skillet over medium heat and sauté onions and peppers for 10 minutes. Add sausage and cayenne and cook until sausage is no longer pink.

Remove from heat; allow to cool. In a mixing bowl, whisk 12 eggs with salt and pepper. Add spinach and combine. Pour meat mixture into egg mixture and combine thoroughly.

Spoon mixture into greased muffin tins. Bake for 20–25 minutes or until a knife inserted in the center comes out clean. Makes approximately 12 muffins.

These are easy and super-yummy. Make them a day ahead for an instant breakfast or snack.

Feel free to add some grated cheese to the mixture if you aren't a strict Paleo eater. My daughters love them with cheese.

Easy Egg Casserole

Similar to egg muffins, this egg casserole is an easy, versatile breakfast that can be made with almost any combination of meat and veggies you have on hand.

Coconut oil to grease baking dish

2   medium, peeled sweet potatoes, sliced thin

1   pound ground beef, turkey, chicken, pork or sausage cooked
in a skillet until browned

2   cups of your choice of chopped veggies (onions, peppers, mushrooms,
zucchini, etc.) that have been sautéed in olive oil

12   eggs

1   teaspoon salt (less if you use ground sausage)

1   teaspoon pepper

1   teaspoon red pepper flakes

Preheat oven to 350 degrees F. Grease a 9×13 baking dish.

Place potatoes on the bottom of the baking dish making sure to cover the dish completely. Use all of the potatoes even if you have to double layer some areas.

Spread cooked, ground meat on the potatoes.

Spread sautéed veggies on top.

Whisk eggs in a bowl with salt, pepper and red pepper flakes. Pour eggs over vegetables.

Bake for about 45 minutes or until firm but not dry. Makes 6 servings.

Apple Muffins

1   ripe banana, peeled
2   apples peeled and finely chopped
⅓   cup water
4   eggs
¼   cup coconut oil, melted
2   cups blanched almond flour
½   teaspoon baking soda
2   heaping tablespoons cinnamon
½   teaspoon nutmeg (optional)

Preheat oven to 350 degrees F.

Mash the banana in a medium bowl.

Add the apples, water, eggs and coconut oil to the bowl and whisk together.

Add almond flour, baking soda, cinnamon and nutmeg (if desired) and mix well. The batter will be thick.

Spoon into greased muffin tins and fill about ¾ full.

Bake for about 15–20 minutes, or until a knife or toothpick inserted in the center of a muffin comes out clean. Let cool for 5 minutes. Makes about 12 muffins.

We like these warm from the oven, but they are also a great snack the next day, especially before a workout.

Breakfast Hash

FRAMPTON FAMILY FAVORITE!

2 medium sweet potatoes, peeled
2 tablespoons ghee (recipe, page 63) or coconut oil, melted
½ pound pork sausage
Sea salt and pepper, to taste
½ teaspoon cinnamon
1 teaspoon ground ginger

Yummy with fried eggs!

Grate the sweet potatoes into a large skillet over medium-high heat with ghee or coconut oil; stir and cook for about 5–10 minutes.

Add the sausage to the skillet and cook another 10–15 minutes until sausage is brown. The potatoes should be tender but beginning to turn brown. Season with salt, pepper, cinnamon and ginger. Makes 4 servings.

Blueberry "Scones"

2½ cups blanched almond flour
½ teaspoon sea salt
1 teaspoon baking soda
½ teaspoon cinnamon
½ cup of ghee (recipe, page 63), melted and cooled
¼ cup of raw honey
2 eggs
1 cup fresh or frozen blueberries

My favorite treat! These come out looking like soft blueberry cookies; they're "buttery" and delicious! Raspberries can be substituted for the blueberries.

Preheat oven to 350 degrees F.

Mix dry ingredients in small bowl and set aside. In a medium bowl, blend ghee, honey and eggs together well. Add the dry mixture to the wet mixture. Gently fold in blueberries. Spoon ¼ cupfuls of mixture onto baking sheet. Bake for about 12–14 minutes. Let rest for 5 minutes and then allow to cool on a cooling rack for 5 minutes more. Makes approximately 12–14 scones.

Sweet Pepper and Onion Frittata

1   onion

1   sweet red bell pepper

4   eggs

½   teaspoon sea salt

½   teaspoon pepper

1   teaspoon garlic powder

1   teaspoon crushed red pepper flakes

2   tablespoons olive oil

Preheat oven to 350 degrees F.

Finely chop onion and pepper. Set aside. Whisk eggs in a small mixing bowl and add salt, pepper, garlic powder and crushed red pepper flakes to taste.

Heat olive oil in the bottom of an ovenproof skillet over medium heat. Add onions and peppers and cook in the hot oil, stirring frequently for about 5 minutes.

Once the onions have started to brown and the peppers are soft, pour eggs over the vegetables and let cook until the edges begin to brown and can be edged away from the sides of the pan with a spatula.

Move the skillet to the oven and bake about 6–8 minutes until the eggs set fully and the top becomes firm to the touch. Makes 2 servings.

Feel free to add sausage or ground beef to this frittata for some extra protein.

Homemade Breakfast Sausage

1	pound ground turkey or pork (or combination of the two)
1	tablespoon garlic powder or 2 garlic cloves, minced
1	tablespoon onion powder
½	teaspoon cumin
½	teaspoon pepper
½	teaspoon nutmeg
½	teaspoon dried oregano
½	teaspoon ground ginger
½	teaspoon dried basil
½	teaspoon ground coriander
½	teaspoon dried sage
1½	teaspoons sea salt
1	egg, lightly beaten

Mix all ingredients together in a large bowl and chill for at least an hour to let the flavors meld. Preheat a skillet over medium heat. Form mixture into patties, about 3 inches in diameter. Add the patties and fry until nicely browned on both sides. Makes about 10–12 patties.

FRAMPTON FAMILY FAVORITE!

These are easy enough to prepare the night before and then toss into a pan with some eggs in the morning for a tasty breakfast. You'll never buy store-bought breakfast sausage again!

SunButter, Chocolate and Banana Pancakes

½   cup SunButter (or any other nut butter that you like)
1   ripe banana, mashed
2   eggs
1   teaspoon vanilla extract
¼   cup chocolate chips (at least 73% cacoa)
Pinch of cinnamon

Combine all ingredients in a bowl and mix well.

Heat a non-stick skillet over medium-high heat (coat with a little coconut oil if needed). Pour the SunButter pancake mix into the skillet to form round pancakes. Cook until you see the bubbles form on top, then flip and cook for about another minute.

Serve as is or with a little maple syrup or honey. Makes 2 servings.

Of all Paleo pancake recipes these are my favorite; I really like the SunButter flavor.

Pumpkin-Pecan Pancakes

½   cup canned pumpkin puree

½   cup almond butter

¼   cup chopped pecans, toasted

2   eggs

2   tablespoons honey

1   teaspoon vanilla

1   teaspoon cinnamon

¼   teaspoon ground nutmeg

Preheat a non-stick skillet over medium-high heat.

Combine all ingredients in a bowl and mix well.

Pour small round pancakes into skillet. Let them cook for about 2–3 minutes; pancakes will start to bubble and cook on the edges.

Flip and cook another minute or two. Makes 2 servings.

These are good with a little maple syrup; the pumpkin and maple go well together.

Paleo Blueberry Pancakes

3   eggs, beaten
1   teaspoon coconut oil, melted
1   teaspoon vanilla extract
2   teaspoons honey or maple syrup (optional)
1   teaspoon cinnamon
½   teaspoon baking soda
2   tablespoons coconut flour
¼   cup fresh or frozen blueberries

Whisk eggs, coconut oil, vanilla and honey in a medium bowl until well-blended. Set aside.

Mix cinnamon, baking soda and coconut flour in a separate bowl. Add wet ingredients to dry ingredients and mix until well-blended. Gently fold in blueberries.

Add additional coconut oil to a large skillet to coat pan. Working in batches if necessary, add batter to make 2-inch pancakes. Cook 3–5 minutes or until bubbles appear on top and edges are cooked. Flip pancakes and cook 1 minute longer.

Serve warm with maple syrup or honey to taste. Makes 2 servings.

Chocolate-Coconut Pancakes

2   eggs, beaten
1   tablespoon unsweetened cocoa powder
½   teaspoon vanilla extract
¼   cup shredded unsweetened coconut flakes
½   cup unsweetened applesauce
¼   cup almond butter
1   teaspoon raw honey
Coconut oil, as needed
Raw honey, maple syrup or fresh berries, if desired

Combine eggs, cocoa, vanilla, coconut, applesauce, almond butter and
1 teaspoon honey in a large bowl and wisk until smooth.

Add a little coconut oil to a large skillet over medium heat. Add batter to
form small pancakes.

Cook for a minute or two and once you see the sides of the pancake starting
to brown, flip the pancake. Once you have flipped the pancake, allow it to
cook for 30 seconds to 1 minute more.

Divide in half, serve hot with honey, maple syrup or berries. Makes 2 servings.

*Let's face it, even the best Paleo pancakes are
not "pancakes" as we know them. Paleo pancakes
are not light and fluffy, but they are healthy
and delicious and will provide you with a sweet
breakfast treat!*

Banana "Oatmeal"

¼ cup walnuts

¼ cup pecans

2 tablespoons of ground flax seed

1 teaspoon of cinnamon or more depending on your taste

¼ teaspoon ground ginger

1 pinch ground nutmeg (optional)

2 eggs

¼ cup of almond or coconut milk

2 ripe bananas, peeled and mashed

2 tablespoons of almond butter or SunButter

¼ cup raisins or berries

Add walnuts, pecans, flax seed, cinnamon, ginger and nutmeg to a food processor and pulse until mixture is the texture of coarse grain. Set aside.

In a large bowl, whisk together eggs and almond milk. In a smaller bowl, blend together mashed banana and almond butter, then add to egg mixture. Mix well.

Using a medium sized saucepan, combine the wet mixture to the dry mixture and stir. Slowly warm the mixture on the stove over medium-low heat until it reaches desired consistency; about 5 minutes. Heat until it reaches preferred thickness.

Mix in raisins or berries. Add a little more almond or coconut milk on the top before serving for added creaminess. Makes 2 servings.

A bowlful of oat-free porridge is a welcome and comforting alternative to eggs and bacon.

Breakfast "Pizza"

1	pound ground mild Italian pork sausage
1	onion, sliced thin
1	sweet bell pepper, chopped
1	cup artichoke hearts, drained and sliced
2	garlic cloves, minced
8	eggs
1	tablespoon dried basil
½	teaspoon sea salt
¼	teaspoon pepper
½	cup tomato sauce
2	tablespoons olive oil
2	tomatoes, sliced

Preheat oven to 350 degrees F.

In a large skillet, brown the sausage over medium-high heat. Remove sausage from skillet. Transfer to a bowl and set aside.

Put onion, pepper, and artichoke hearts in skillet and sauté for about 10 minutes until vegetables are soft and beginning to brown. Add garlic and sauté for 2 additional minutes. Transfer to a bowl and set aside.

Whisk eggs in a bowl with basil, salt and pepper.

In a large skillet, heat the olive oil over medium heat and pour the egg mixture into the skillet. Cover and let cook for about 3 minutes, or until the bottom of the eggs are set and firm. Do not stir the eggs while cooking.

Uncover the lid and transfer the skillet to the oven and broil for about 3 minutes, until browned on top. Remove from the oven and spread evenly the tomato sauce, the cooked sausage, and the rest of the toppings.

Place the pizza back in the oven and broil for another 5 minutes. Remove from oven, cut into slices and serve immediately. Makes 4 servings.

Steak and Mushroom Frittata

1   tablespoon coconut or olive oil
1   sweet onion, thinly sliced
1   red bell pepper, thinly sliced
1   package mushrooms, sliced
3   garlic cloves, minced
1   jalapeño pepper, seeded and minced
½   pound steak, cooked and thinly sliced
12 eggs
½   teaspoon dried thyme
Ground pepper

Preheat oven to 375 degrees F.

Heat the oil in a large ovenproof skillet over medium-high heat. Add onion, pepper, mushrooms, garlic and jalapeño and sauté for 10 minutes. Add the steak.

While the vegetables cook, whisk the eggs in a large bowl. Add thyme and pepper. Pour the egg mixture on top of the steak and vegetables.

Place the skillet in the oven and cook for 25–30 minutes or until mixture has set.

Note: If you want the top a little crispy, set oven to broil for the last few minutes. Let rest for 5 minutes before slicing. Makes 4 servings.

Banana Nut Muffins

1	cup unsweetened shredded coconut
2	tablespoons blanched almond flour
2	eggs
½	cup walnuts or pecans, chopped
2	teaspoons coconut oil
2	teaspoons almond butter
3	tablespoons honey
4	bananas, mashed

Preheat oven to 375 degrees F.

Mix all ingredients thoroughly in a bowl then pour into greased muffin tins.

Bake for about 20–25 minutes or until a toothpick inserted in the center of a muffin comes out clean. Makes about 10 muffins.

FRAMPTON FAMILY FAVORITE!

Ben's Banana and Blueberry-Nut Muffins

2   cups blanched almond flour

1   teaspoon baking powder

1   teaspoon baking soda

⅛   teaspoon salt

2   bananas, peeled and mashed

¼   cup applesauce

3   eggs

¼   cup honey

1   teaspoon vanilla extract

1   cup blueberries

½   cup walnuts, chopped

Preheat oven to 350 degrees F.

Mix flour, baking powder, baking soda and salt in a bowl and set aside.

Mix bananas, applesauce, eggs, honey, and vanilla in a separate bowl.

Add wet ingredients to dry ingredients and mix well.

Fold in blueberries and walnuts (or any nut of your choice) and mix.

Pour batter into greased muffin tins.

Bake for 20–25 minutes or until a toothpick inserted in the center of a muffin comes out clean. Makes about 12 muffins.

This recipe was submitted by friend and fellow CrossFitter, Ben Rotker.

Breakfast Squash

1   delicata squash, cut in half and seeded
1   tablespoon coconut oil, melted
½   teaspoon sea salt
Pepper, to taste
½   teaspoon cinnamon
1   teaspoon ground coriander
½   pound ground pork sausage
1   sweet onion, chopped
Red pepper flakes
4   eggs

Preheat oven to 400 degrees F.

Place squash in a large baking dish, skin-side down, and spread the coconut oil over the two squash halves. Sprinkle with salt, pepper, cinnamon and coriander. Bake until squash is tender, about 15–20 minutes.

While squash is roasting, brown sausage, onion and red pepper flakes in a skillet and set aside.

Remove squash from oven.

Turn oven temperature down to 375 degrees F.

Fill each squash with the browned sausage and onion mixture. Place stuffed squash halves cut-side-up in the baking dish. Top with whisked eggs and transfer back to the oven.

Bake until eggs are puffed slightly and cooked through, about 10 minutes. Makes 2 servings.

Live your life as healthy as possible.

Appetizers

I love food you can eat with your hands, which is why appetizers are so appealing. Occasionally we have "appetizer dinner nights" when each family member chooses one or more favorite appetizer. Then we share a fine assortment of finger-friendly foods.

Try one or try all. But most importantly, have fun doing it!

Spicy Chicken and Bacon Bites

2　large boneless, skinless chicken breasts, cut in 1-inch pieces

Sea salt and pepper, to taste

2　tablespoons coconut oil, melted

1　pound bacon (try to get thin sliced, it works better)

Preheat the grill to medium.

Season the chicken pieces with salt, pepper and coconut oil. Wrap each piece of chicken with approximately ½ slice of bacon; try to wrap tightly and secure with a skewer (wooden or metal). If you use the wooden skewers, remember to soak them in water for about 10 minutes before using.

Over medium heat, grill all of the chicken/bacon pieces until bacon is crisp and chicken is cooked, about 10–15 minutes total, flipping on the grill a couple of times. Makes 4 servings.

Almond-Stuffed Dates

15-20　Medjool dates, pitted

15-20　raw whole almonds

Roast the almonds in a dry skillet over medium–high heat, stirring them frequently for about 5 minutes. Make sure the almonds don't burn.

Cool the nuts and then stuff one into each date. Serve. Makes 6 servings.

We like to make a dessert out of these by dipping them in melted dark chocolate and then chilling them for about an hour.

Plantain Chips and Dip

4   avocados

1   medium tomato, finely chopped

Juice of 1 lime

½   teaspoon salt

1   garlic clove, minced

½   teaspoon pepper

3   ripe plantains (they are ripe when they look black and rotten)

¼   cup coconut oil

Mash the avocados and add tomato, lime juice, salt, garlic and pepper. Mix well and chill while preparing the plantains.

Leave the peel on the plantain and cut off the ends. Slice the plantain in half and then as thin as possible lengthwise. Leaving the peel on while slicing will help prevent smashing the plantain.

After the plantains are sliced, remove the peel and place the sliced plantains into a skillet of hot coconut oil. Fry for about 2 minutes on each side; be careful not to burn them but try to get them as crispy as possible.

Transfer to a paper towel and add salt to taste. Serve with avocado dip. Makes 6 servings.

You can't control everything that happens to you, but you can control what you put into your body.

Guacamole Tomatoes

4   avocados, peeled, pitted and chopped

½   cup onion, chopped fine

1   tablespoon garlic powder

1   teaspoon pepper

Hot sauce, to taste

Juice of 1 lime

15-20 cherry tomatoes (try to find the larger sized tomatoes, they're easier to work with)

1   bunch cilantro, leaves removed and finely chopped

In a bowl, combine avocado, onion, garlic powder, pepper, hot sauce and lime juice. Mix well and place in the refrigerator while you prepare the tomatoes.

Cut the tops off the tomatoes and hollow them out (use a melon baller if you have it; it works well to accomplish this task). Make sure they are completely empty.

Place all tomatoes with the cut-side-down on a paper towel to drain excess tomato juice. Let drain for 5 minutes. Turn tomatoes cut-side-up and mound the guacamole into each tomato.

Place enough guacamole in each tomato so that they are a bit overflowing.

Once all of the tomatoes are filled, sprinkle the cilantro on top and serve! Makes 4 servings.

Make sure to give your body the rest it deserves; adequate sleep is essential to good health.

Chicken "Fingers"

½   cup almond flour

1   teaspoon sea salt

½   teaspoon dried basil

½   teaspoon dried thyme

½   teaspoon ground ginger

1   teaspoon dry mustard powder

⅓   cup coconut oil for frying

2   boneless, skinless chicken breasts, sliced into finger-sized lengths

1   egg, beaten

Mix the almond flour, salt, basil, thyme, ginger and mustard in a bowl.

Heat the oil in a large skillet over medium-high heat.

Put the beaten egg in one bowl and the almond flour mixture into another bowl. Dip each chicken finger in egg, then in the almond flour mixture.

Cook in skillet for about 3 minutes each side or until thoroughly cooked but not dry.

Serve alone or with a dipping sauce of choice. Makes 4 servings.

You'll never reach for store-bought chicken fingers ever again!

Kale Chips

1   bunch kale, washed, dried and cut into pieces about the size
of the palm of your hand
2   tablespoons olive oil
¼   teaspoon sea salt

Preheat oven to 350 degrees F.

Place kale on a baking sheet. Toss the kale with oil and salt.

Bake for 10–15 minutes or until kale is dark green and crispy, stirring half way through.

Cool and serve. Makes 4 servings.

You can add other flavors or seasonings to your kale chips. Try:
- *2 tablespoons lemon juice or*
- *2 tablespoons vinegar or*
- *garlic salt or garlic powder*

Get creative and enjoy; these are addictive!

When your ten-year-old says, "Weird. These taste just like chips," you know you have a winner on your hands!

Sweet Potato Chips

3 large sweet potatoes
3-4 tablespoons coconut oil, melted
Sea salt and pepper, to taste

Preheat oven to 375 degrees F.

Wash and peel the sweet potatoes. Thinly slice the sweet potatoes using a mandolin or by hand.

Coat the baking sheet with coconut oil. Brush the sliced sweet potatoes liberally with more coconut oil.

Bake for 20 minutes, turning at least once. They are ready when they turn golden brown. Add salt and pepper, to taste. Let cool for 10 minutes on a wire rack, which will help make them crispier. Makes 4 servings.

Spicy Salsa

6 large tomatoes, chopped
(drain about ½ the juice from the chopped tomatoes)
1 small red onion, finely diced
3 garlic cloves, minced
1 cucumber, finely diced
1 red bell pepper, finely chopped
Juice of 1 lime
1 jalapeño pepper, seeded and finely diced
½ cup fresh cilantro, chopped
Sea salt and pepper, to taste

Mix all ingredients in a bowl. Serve.
Makes 4 servings.

This salsa is great as a side dish with grilled meats, especially a nice, spicy flank steak.

Spicy Guacamole

4   large avocados
1   tomato, chopped
½   red onion, diced fine
3   garlic cloves, minced
1   tablespoon crushed red pepper flakes
Pepper, to taste
Juice of 1 lime
1   bunch cilantro, leaves removed and finely chopped

Pit, halve and scoop avocados into bowl and mash. Mix all ingredients into mashed avocados to preferred consistency (smooth or chunky).

Let chill for half hour and serve. Makes 4 servings.

This is also great on top of burgers, chicken breasts or fish!

Spicy Mango Salsa

6   tomatoes, chopped (drain at least ½ of the tomato juice)

3   ripe mangos, peeled and cut into small pieces

1   red bell pepper, chopped

1   orange bell pepper, chopped

2   jalapeño peppers, seeded and minced

1   serrano pepper, seeded and minced

1   sweet onion, finely chopped

½   jicama, peeled and chopped

3   garlic cloves, minced

Juice from 2 limes

2   tablespoons olive oil

Sea salt and pepper, to taste

1   bunch cilantro, leaves removed and finely chopped

Mix tomatoes, mango, all peppers, onion, jicama and garlic in a large bowl.

Squeeze limes over mixture, add olive oil, and mix well.

Season with salt and pepper to taste.

Add cilantro and serve. Makes 4 servings.

Substitute one pineapple (peeled and diced) for the mango and you have another sweet-tasting salsa!

Baba Ghanoush

1   large eggplant
2   tablespoons olive oil
1   garlic clove, minced
1   teaspoon salt
½   cup tahini
½   teaspoon cumin
1   tablespoon lemon juice
1   tablespoon fresh parsley, roughly chopped

Preheat oven to 350 degrees F.

Peel eggplant and cut into 1-inch chunks. Place on baking sheet and toss with olive oil.

Bake for about 30–40 minutes or until soft and slightly brown. Remove from oven and cool.

Place eggplant in food processor. Add garlic, salt, tahini, cumin, lemon juice and parsley. Blend to a smooth puree.

Serve with veggies. Makes 4 servings.

Baba Ganoush is a great topping for burgers, fish or grilled chicken.

Spicy Grilled Shrimp

2   pounds raw shrimp, peeled and deveined

2   tablespoons of Emeril's Essence seasoning or use the Cajun Rub recipe, page 71

2   tablespoons olive oil

Preheat grill to medium.

Mix all ingredients in a large Ziploc bag and marinate in refrigerator for about 30 minutes.

Skewer the shrimp and grill 2 minutes, flip and cook another minute or so until shrimp are pink. Makes 6 servings.

Delicious.

Bacon-Wrapped Sweet Potato Fries

2   sweet potatoes, cut into 6 pieces each by slicing lengthwise

1   pound thinly sliced bacon

Juice of 1 lime

Preheat oven to 425 degrees F.

Slice each piece of bacon in half, lengthwise. Wrap 1 strip of bacon around 1 piece of sweet potato. Place in one layer on a jelly-roll pan. Repeat until all the bacon is gone.

If you have left over sweet potatoes, place them on the pan too, and they'll cook up nicely in the bacon fat.

Bake fries for about 45 minutes, turning a couple times during baking. You want the bacon to look brown and crispy.

Enjoy by themselves or with dip of choice. Makes 4 servings.

These are also great as a side dish!

Dressings, Marinades, Rubs and Sauces

So versatile! So flavorful! This collection of recipes proves that a simple cut of meat (or fish) can be altered in seconds with a drizzle of a sauce. Tired of the same marinade you always use? Try one, two or all listed here. Don't be afraid to try new flavors or to use these recipes in different ways. For example, a rub meant for a flank steak can be a delicious addition to ground beef. A dressing can become a marinade. Add your favorite spices and herbs to make a dish "yours." This section is where flavors happen; experiment and enjoy!

Basic Vinaigrette

¼   cup vinegar: red wine, cider, or balsamic
(you may also use lemon or lime juice instead)
1   tablespoon shallots, chopped
2   teaspoons Dijon mustard
½   teaspoon sea salt
¼   teaspoon pepper
½   cup olive oil

Mix the first 5 ingredients in a food processor. With the machine running, slowly add the olive oil down the feed tube and process until the mixture has emulsified. Whisk in a bowl or shake in a jar before using. Makes 2–4 servings.

Make yourself a priority. Make your diet a priority!

Italian Vinaigrette

¼   cup red wine vinegar
⅓   cup olive oil
Sea salt and pepper, to taste
1   garlic clove, minced
1   tablespoon dried basil
1   teaspoon dried oregano

Whisk all ingredients in a bowl or a jar. Whisk or shake well before using. Makes 2–4 servings.

Fresh Tomato Vinaigrette

2   large, ripe tomatoes, finely chopped
1   garlic clove, minced
1   tablespoon red wine vinegar
2   tablespoons olive oil
1   tablespoon fresh or ½ teaspoon dried basil
Sea salt and pepper, to taste

Mix all ingredients well in a bowl or jar. Whisk or shake before using.
Makes 2–4 servings.

This is outstanding when made with garden-fresh summer tomatoes!

Pomegranate Vinaigrette

1   tablespoon shallots, finely chopped
1   tablespoon pomegranate molasses
(available in big supermarkets or Middle Eastern shops)
1   tablespoon balsamic vinegar
2   teaspoons lemon juice
1   teaspoon dried tarragon
¼   teaspoon sea salt
¼   cup olive oil
2   teaspoons water

Mix shallots, pomegranate molasses, vinegar, lemon juice, tarragon and salt in a bowl.

Whisk in oil, and then add water. Whisk to blend before using.
Makes 2–4 servings.

Creamy Citrus Dressing

1 avocado, peeled and pitted
½ cup fresh-squeezed orange Juice
¼ cup fresh lime juice
1 bunch cilantro, leaves removed and finely chopped
1 onion, chopped
1 tablespoon shallots, chopped
½ jalapeño pepper, seeded and chopped
½ teaspoon sea salt
Pepper, to taste
½ cup olive oil
2 teaspoons water

Blend all of the ingredients except oil and water in a food processor until smooth. With the machine running, add oil slowly down the feed tube and process until emulsified. The dressing will be thick and creamy. Add water and pulse to blend.

Adjust any of the ingredients to suit your taste. If dressing is too thick add a little more water. Makes 4 servings.

Cilantro-Lime Dressing

¼ cup cider vinegar
Juice of 1 lime
¼ cup cilantro, leaves removed and finely chopped
1 teaspoon sea salt
1 teaspoon pepper
1 cup olive oil

Mix all ingredients except olive oil in a food processor. With the machine running, add oil slowly down the feed tube until emulsified. Makes 4 servings.

Lemon and Mustard Vinaigrette

3 tablespoons olive oil
Juice of 1 lemon
Juice of ½ orange
1 tablespoon grainy mustard
Sea salt and pepper, to taste

Mix all ingredients in a jar and shake well to mix before using.
Makes 2 servings.

Creamy Garlic and Avocado Dressing

2 avocados, peeled and pitted
Juice of 1 lemon
⅓ cup coconut milk, or more to taste
3 garlic cloves
Sea salt and pepper, to taste
¼ teaspoon dried tarragon
½ teaspoon dried thyme

Mix all ingredients well in food processor or blender. Makes 4 servings.

Citrus and Garlic Dressing

3   tablespoons olive oil

1   tablespoon balsamic vinegar

Juice of ½ lemon or lime

2   garlic cloves, minced

Sea salt and pepper, to taste

Mix all ingredients in a jar and shake well before using. Makes 2 servings.

Move your body every day!

Avocado Dressing

2   ripe avocados, peeled and pitted

⅓   cup olive oil

2   garlic cloves

2   tablespoons lemon juice

½   teaspoon pepper

Pinch of cayenne pepper

½   teaspoon sea salt

½   cup roasted red and yellow peppers

(you can roast peppers yourself or use jarred peppers)

Place all ingredients in a food processor and blend until smooth.
Makes 4 servings.

Ghee (Clarified Butter)

To make ghee (clarified butter), melt unsalted butter in a saucepan over low heat until the butter separates into 3 layers; the top layer will be white foam. The milk solids will drop to the bottom of the saucepan and form a layer of sediment. What is left in the middle is a pure golden-yellow liquid called clarified butter. To extract the clarified butter, skim off and discard the top layer of foam. Once foam has been discarded, remove the saucepan from the heat.

Let the clarified butter sit a few minutes to allow the milk solids to settle to the bottom, and then strain the mixture over a bowl through a fine sieve, cheesecloth or paper towel-lined strainer. The liquid collected is the clarified butter, ghee.

Make a ghee and coconut oil combination by measuring the clarified butter then add an equal quantity of melted (cooled slightly) coconut oil. Mix well and store in a glass container (such as a canning jar). Cover tightly and store at room temperature up to 3 months or longer.

Be very careful not to overheat the butter as it melts; if overheated, it can become bitter-tasting.

Pistachio Salsa

½   cup toasted pistachios, roughly chopped
1   tomato, finely diced
⅓   cup fresh parsley, chopped
1   garlic clove, minced
1   tablespoon lemon juice
½   teaspoon ground paprika

Mix all ingredients in a bowl until blended. Makes 2 servings.

This is great on cooked fish or chicken.

Tangy "Peanut" Sauce

½   cup almond butter

¼   cup lime juice

2   teaspoons fish sauce

2   teaspoons dark sesame oil

2   teaspoons red wine vinegar

2   teaspoons agave

¼   cup water

¼   cup cilantro, leaves removed and finely chopped

2   garlic cloves, minced

2   teaspoons fresh ginger, finely chopped

1   teaspoon chili powder

Combine almond butter, lime juice, fish sauce, sesame oil, vinegar, agave and water in a jar and shake well to mix.

Add cilantro, garlic, ginger and chili powder and shake again before serving. Makes 4 servings.

Tart Cranberry Sauce

1   pound fresh cranberries

½   cup orange juice

½   cup water

1   tablespoon raw honey

Rinse cranberries in a colander.

Place cranberries, orange juice and water in a large, heavy sauce pan and bring to a boil, stirring occasionally. After boiling a few minutes, cranberries will begin to pop open. Continue to stir.

Once most of them have popped, stir in the honey. Remove from heat and cool. Makes 4 servings.

Spinach Pesto

1   (16 ounce) bag of baby spinach
1   cup of fresh basil
½   cup walnuts or pine nuts
1   garlic clove, peeled
½   teaspoon sea salt
⅓   cup olive oil

Place the spinach and basil in a food processor and pulse to a coarse paste.

Add walnuts or pines nuts, garlic and salt and pulse until smooth. With the machine running, slowly add the olive oil down the feed tube and process until the mixture has emulsified. Season with salt to taste. Makes 6 servings.

Add to warm vegetables or top your protein.

Basil Pesto

2   cups packed fresh basil leaves
¼   cup pine nuts, toasted (or substitute cashews or walnuts)
3   garlic cloves
½   cup olive oil
½   cup grated parmesan cheese (optional)
Sea salt and pepper, to taste

Put the basil, garlic and nuts in a food processor and pulse until everything is finely chopped. Add the olive oil and parmesan (if using) and pulse again until smooth.

Season to taste with salt and pepper. Makes 6 servings.

Pesto freezes well. Make an extra batch for later.

Chimichurri Sauce

½   red onion, coarsely chopped
4   garlic cloves
1   cup fresh cilantro
½   cup fresh parsley
Juice of 1 lime
¾   cup olive oil
1   teaspoon sea salt
Pepper, to taste

Place all ingredients in a food processor and pulse on low until the mixture is almost smooth (it should still be a bit chunky). Makes 4 servings.

Cashew Hummus

1½ cups raw cashews
¼   cup tahini
¼   cup lemon juice
1   small garlic clove
½   teaspoon sea salt

Place all ingredients in a food processor and pulse until smooth. Add extra lemon juice or water to desired thickness. Makes 4 servings.

If you have time, toast the cashews in a skillet over low heat for a few minutes, stirring frequently, before using them in this recipe.

Beet Hummus

4	medium sized beets, boiled, peeled and cubed
¼	cup tahini
¼	cup lemon juice
1	small garlic clove
½	teaspoon sea salt

Beets are my favorite vegetable... and this hummus is amazing!

Place all ingredients in a food processor and pulse until smooth. Add extra lemon juice or water to desired thickness and tanginess. Makes 4 servings.

Basic Mayonnaise

2	egg yolks (use pasteurized egg yolks, if possible)
1	teaspoon Dijon mustard
4	teaspoons fresh lemon juice
1	cup olive oil

Sea salt and pepper, to taste

In a food processor, combine egg yolks, Dijon mustard and lemon juice. Pulse until well combined. With the machine running, slowly add the oil down the feed tube and process until the mixture has emulsified. The mixture should be thick. Season with salt and pepper. Makes approximately 1½ cups.

Flavor-up your mayonnaise! I never eat it plain. Some of my favorite additions:
- *Cilantro and lime juice*
- *Basil and additional lemon juice*
- *Minced garlic*
- *Pureed red pepper*

Garlic and Herb Marinade

½   cup red onion, finely chopped
1   teaspoon dried thyme
1   teaspoon dried marjoram
1   teaspoon sea salt
½   cup olive oil
¼   cup lemon juice
1   tablespoon dried parsley
1   garlic clove, minced
½   teaspoon pepper

Combine all ingredients in a medium bowl or a Ziploc bag. Coat steak or chicken with the marinade for at least 2 hours or overnight. If you use this to marinate fish, do not marinate more than 2 hours. Makes enough to marinate 1–2 pounds of meat or fish.

Fajita Marinade

½   cup olive oil
⅓   cup lime juice
¼   cup vinegar
½   teaspoon sea salt
2   teaspoons raw honey
½   cup onion, finely chopped
3   garlic cloves, minced
½   tablespoon paprika
1   teaspoon dried oregano
½   teaspoon ground cumin
½   teaspoon pepper

Combine the marinade ingredients in a medium bowl or a large Ziploc bag. Add beef, chicken or fish and marinate for 2 hours or overnight for beef and chicken. Makes enough to marinate up to 2 pounds.

Basic Chili Rub

2 tablespoons chili powder

1 tablespoon garlic powder

1 teaspoon sea salt

1 teaspoon pepper

Mix all the spices together in a small bowl and generously rub on beef, chicken or fish. Makes enough to season 2 pounds of meat.

Taco Seasoning

2 tablespoons chili powder

½ teaspoon garlic powder

½ teaspoon onion powder

½ teaspoon crushed red pepper flakes

½ teaspoon dried oregano

2 teaspoons paprika

1 teaspoon ground cumin

1 teaspoon sea salt

1 teaspoon pepper

Mix together all ingredients and use as a traditional taco seasoning. Add to ground beef or ground turkey. Makes enough to season 2 pounds of meat.

My kids love this taco seasoning; it's better than any packaged, high-sodium brand on the market.

Chili Seasoning

2   tablespoons chili powder
1   tablespoon crushed red pepper
1   tablespoon onion powder
1   tablespoon garlic powder
2   teaspoons ground cumin
2   teaspoons dried parsley
2   teaspoons salt
½   teaspoon pepper

Mix all seasonings together in a small bowl, jar or Ziploc bag.
Makes enough to season 2 pounds of meat.

Citrus Marinade

¼   cup lemon juice
3   tablespoons lime juice
¼   teaspoon lemon pepper
2   garlic cloves, minced
½   cup olive oil
1   teaspoon dried basil

Combine all ingredients in a small bowl. Coat pork, chicken or fish
with the marinade and let it stand at room temperature for 1 hour (for
fish) or in the refrigerator for up to 4 hours if using pork or chicken.
Makes enough to marinate 1–2 pounds of meat or fish.

The fresh taste of lemon and lime juices are delicious with pork, chicken or fish.

Cajun Seasoning

1   tablespoon mustard powder
1   tablespoon ground cumin
2   teaspoons celery seeds
1½ teaspoons pepper
1   teaspoon sea salt
2   teaspoons coconut crystals
½   teaspoon cayenne pepper
2   tablespoons olive oil

Combine all the ingredients except olive oil in a small bowl. Set aside.

Coat chicken, beef or fish with the olive oil and then rub seasoning mixture over generously. Makes enough to season 1–2 pounds of meat or fish.

You can change your diet. You will feel better if you do!

Mark Sisson's Primal 51 Ketchup

1   (6 ounce) can tomato paste
⅔   cup cider vinegar
⅓   cup water
3   tablespoons raw honey or pure maple syrup
3   tablespoons chopped onion
2   garlic cloves
1   teaspoon sea salt
⅛   teaspoon ground allspice
⅛   teaspoon ground cloves, optional
⅛   teaspoon pepper

Mix all ingredients in a food processor until smooth. Add more water if it's too thick.

Store ketchup in a tightly covered jar or glass container in the refrigerator for up to 3 weeks. Makes approximately 1½ cups.

This ketchup is so good! My kids love it. I omit the cloves, but that's just my personal preference.

Mark Sisson's BBQ Sauce

1   cup homemade Primal 51 Ketchup (recipe, page 72)

3   tablespoons minced onion

3   tablespoons ghee (recipe, page 63)

2   tablespoons orange juice, freshly squeezed

¼   cup pure maple syrup

2   tablespoons Worcestershire sauce

1   tablespoon chili powder

1   tablespoon unfiltered cider vinegar

2   teaspoons molasses

1   teaspoon sea salt

Mix all ingredients together in a small pan and simmer over low heat for 10–15 minutes, stirring occasionally.

Cool. Store the BBQ sauce in airtight glass container in the refrigerator for up to 3 weeks. Makes approximately 1½ cups.

All I can say is, YUMMY! Thank you Mark!

Soups and Salads

My family loves soup in winter and cool salads all summer long. During the cold months, Sunday nights mean soup at the Frampton house. When warmer weather rolls around, we eat salads out on the pool deck until the days grow cool again. Soups and salads are such easy meals to create. Prepare soups by following specific recipes or just throw what you have into a pot with some stock and seasonings. Always make enough to freeze for another meal. Salads are just as versatile. Mix in whatever greens you have with fresh vegetables, and top with your favorite protein and dressing. Done!

Beet, Jicama and Avocado Salad

2   cups beets, boiled, peeled and cut into ½-inch dice

1   jicama, peeled and cut into ½-inch dice

4   radishes, grated

2   avocados, peeled, pitted and sliced into 1-inch pieces

½   cup fresh cilantro, chopped

2   tablespoons lemon juice

½   teaspoon ground cumin

½   teaspoon ground coriander

½   teaspoon sea salt or more to taste

2   tablespoons olive oil

½   teaspoon pepper

Mix beets, jicama, and radishes together in a large bowl.

Gently add avocado and cilantro. Set aside. (Note: avocados turn brown quickly, so add them just before dressing and serving.)

Whisk together lemon juice, cumin, coriander, salt and pepper in a medium bowl. While whisking constantly, add the oil slowly until dressing has emulsified.

Pour over beet mixture and mix gently to blend. Add more salt or pepper, if desired. Makes 4 servings.

FRAMPTON FAMILY FAVORITE! (MOSTLY MOM)

Cumin can sometimes overtake other flavors; use it wisely. If you like the flavor, use it liberally.

Winter Salad with Roasted Squash

1   medium butternut squash, peeled, seeded and diced

2   teaspoons olive oil

1   teaspoon thyme

Sea salt and pepper, to taste

2   cups romaine hearts, torn into pieces

2   cups baby spinach

¼   cup Pomegranate Vinaigrette (recipe, page 59)

¼   cup pomegranate seeds

2   tablespoons coarsely chopped pistachios or walnuts, toasted

Heat oven to 375 degrees F.

Place squash in a large baking dish, drizzle with oil, and toss to coat. Spread in one or two large baking dishes in a single layer and sprinkle with thyme. Season with salt and pepper.

Bake, stirring once or twice, until the squash is tender, about 25 minutes. Let cool.

Place lettuce, spinach, and squash in a bowl. Add vinaigrette and gently toss to blend.

Sprinkle with pomegranate seeds and toasted nuts. Makes 4 servings.

This is such a wonderful combination of warm and cool vegetables. The simple flavors are perfect together.

Asparagus and Red Pepper Salad

6   tablespoons olive oil

1   red bell pepper, cut into 1-inch pieces

1   pound asparagus, ends trimmed and chopped into 1-inch pieces

1   shallot, minced

1   tablespoon sherry vinegar or wine vinegar

1   garlic clove, minced

1   (12 ounce) bag of baby spinach

½   teaspoon sea salt

½   teaspoon pepper

Heat 2 tablespoons of the olive oil in large skillet over medium-high heat. Add the red peppers and cook for 2 minutes.

Add the asparagus, salt, and pepper and sauté for about another 5 minutes or until asparagus is crisp-tender.

Reduce heat to medium and add shallots. Cook another 2 minutes then remove from heat.

Whisk together remaining 4 tablespoons of oil, vinegar, and garlic in a medium bowl and add salt and pepper to taste. Mix a little more than half the dressing with the baby spinach in a serving bowl.

Top spinach with asparagus and pepper mixture, and drizzle remaining dressing on top. Makes 4 servings.

FRAMPTON FAMILY FAVORITE! (MOSTLY MOM)

This recipe was inspired by a similar salad served by our friends, the Conleys.

Beet Salad

3-4 medium-sized beets
½ red onion, chopped fine
1 fennel bulb, halved, stem and fronds removed, thinly sliced
Grated zest of 1 lemon
Juice of ½ lemon
1-2 tablespoons olive oil
¼ teaspoon sea salt
¼ teaspoon pepper

My favorite! I could have this salad several times a week and never complain. I love beets!

Trim stalks from the beets. Cook beets in boiling salted water until tender, about 20-30 minutes.

Drain beets, cool until easy to handle, then use paper towels to help remove the peel. Cut beets into 1-inch pieces; chill in the refrigerator 30 minutes or until cool.

Combine beets, onion and fennel in a large bowl.

Whisk lemon zest, juice, olive oil, salt, and pepper together in a small bowl. Pour over beet mixture and toss. Makes 4 servings.

Carrot Salad

6 large carrots, peeled and grated
2-3 tablespoons fresh parsley, finely chopped
1 tablespoon lemon juice
2 tablespoons olive oil
1 garlic clove, minced
½ teaspoon ground cumin
½ teaspoon sea salt
¼ teaspoon pepper

Simple and fresh! Blend in a bit of Basic Mayonnaise (page 67) if you like traditional carrot salad.

Combine all ingredients in a large bowl and mix well. Makes 4 servings.

Caramelized Onion and Sweet Potato Salad

4   tablespoons coconut oil
3   sweet onions, thinly sliced
1   tablespoon Dijon mustard
¼   cup balsamic vinegar
2   teaspoons raw honey
1   tablespoon grated lemon zest
1   teaspoon dried thyme
3   medium sweet potatoes, sliced into ½-inch slices
Sea salt and pepper, to taste

Heat 2 tablespoons of coconut oil in a skillet over medium heat. Cook onions slowly—about 15 minutes—until golden brown and caramelized.

Add mustard and vinegar and cook for another 5–10 minutes.

Remove from heat. Add honey, lemon zest, and thyme. Mix well and let cool.

Preheat oven to 400 degrees F.

Place the potatoes in one layer in a large baking pan. Brush the potato slices on both sides generously with the remaining coconut oil and season with salt and pepper. Roast the potatoes 5–10 minutes on each side or until tender but not mushy.

Place potatoes in a bowl and gently mix in onion mixture. Serve warm. Makes 4 servings.

Strawberry Salad

3   tablespoons raspberry balsamic vinegar

1   teaspoon raw honey

1½   teaspoons Dijon mustard

½   cup of olive oil

4   cups mixed greens or lettuce of choice

8   fresh strawberries, hulled and thinly sliced

¼   cup walnuts or pecans, chopped

Whisk vinegar, honey, Dijon mustard and olive oil in a bowl until well-blended. Set aside.

Place mixed greens in a serving bowl with sliced strawberries and chopped nuts. Drizzle with raspberry vinaigrette, lightly toss, and serve. Makes 4 servings.

FRAMPTON FAMILY FAVORITE!

Feel free to substitute raspberries for strawberries; both versions are great!

Warm Arugula Salad

1   (16 ounce) bag of arugula
6   strips bacon, chopped
2   shallots, finely chopped
2   tablespoons olive oil
Pepper, to taste
Handful of chopped walnuts
*Add any other vegetables you'd like

Place the arugula in a large salad bowl and set aside.

In a large skillet cook the chopped bacon until crisp. Drain on paper towels and set aside. Add the shallots to the bacon fat and cook, stirring frequently, over medium heat 10 minutes or until the shallots are translucent. Transfer the shallots to a small bowl and set aside. Discard half of the bacon fat or reserve it for another use.

Add the olive oil to the bacon fat in the skillet and heat another 2 minutes. Remove from heat and let cool for 2 minutes.

Pour the olive oil, bacon and shallots over the arugula and mix well. The heat from the mixture will wilt the arugula slightly. Add fresh ground black pepper and walnuts and serve immediately. Makes 4 servings.

FRAMPTON FAMILY FAVORITE!

You can substitute turkey sausage for the bacon. No shallots on hand? Use minced sweet or red onion instead.

The warm, wilted arugula is so good. We often throw any leftover vegetables from the previous night's dinner right on top of this salad.

Mixed Greens and Sausage Salad

1   (16 ounce) bag mixed greens

2   medium seedless cucumbers, chopped into bite-sized pieces

1   avocado, peeled, pitted and sliced

3   tomatoes, sliced or chopped into 1-inch pieces

1   red bell pepper, chopped into bite-sized pieces

1   package sausage (any kind you like; we love apple chicken sausages in this)

3   tablespoons olive oil

1   tablespoon balsamic vinegar

Juice of ½ lemon or lime

2   garlic cloves, minced

Sea salt and pepper, to taste

Preheat grill to medium.

Combine greens, cucumbers, avocado, tomatoes and peppers in a large bowl and set aside.

Grill sausage until cooked through. Cut sausage into pieces and set aside.

Whisk together olive oil, vinegar, lemon juice, garlic, salt and pepper in a medium bowl. Drizzle dressing onto the salad and mix thoroughly.

Add sausage to salad. Makes 4 servings.

FRAMPTON FAMILY FAVORITE!

Great salad! We also love it with grilled steak tips.

Cobb Salad

Juice of 1 lemon

1   egg (preferably pasteurized), beaten

2   garlic cloves, minced

2-3 tablespoons Dijon mustard

1   tablespoon fresh dill, chopped, or 1 teaspoon dried dill

Pepper, to taste

Pinch of cayenne pepper

¼   cup olive oil

½   cup coconut milk

4   eggs, hard-boiled and sliced

10   slices bacon, cooked and crumbled

1   (16 ounce) bag of mixed greens (you may use romaine)

2   large avocados, peeled, pitted and sliced

2   tomatoes, diced

2   cooked chicken breasts, shredded

Several slices nitrate-free ham, chopped

Handful of walnuts or slivered almonds

Dressing:
Whisk lemon juice, egg, garlic, mustard, dill, pepper and cayenne in a medium bowl. While whisking constantly, slowly add the olive oil and coconut milk.

Salad:
Arrange all greens and vegetables on a large platter and toss with dressing. Top with eggs, bacon and meats. Sprinkle with walnuts or almonds and fresh dill. Makes 6 servings.

This is a great salad because you can prep most things the night before and throw it together the next day for a quick dinner. The dressing is nice and creamy. Play around with the ingredients to reach a consistency that you like, adding more or less lemon juice or coconut milk.

Taco Salad with Guacamole

4 fresh avocados, peeled, pitted and mashed

1-2 garlic cloves, minced

¼ cup red onion, finely diced

Juice of 2 limes

¼ teaspoon ground cumin

1 teaspoon chili powder

1 teaspoon sea salt

Pepper, to taste

1 jalapeño pepper, seeded and finely chopped

1 small bunch of cilantro, leaves removed and finely chopped

2 pounds ground beef

1 (16 ounce) can diced tomatoes with their juices

1 tablespoon paprika

1 tablespoon chili powder

½ teaspoon ground cumin

1 head of romaine lettuce, chopped

1 yellow bell pepper, diced

1 red bell pepper, diced

1 jar of salsa or Spicy Salsa (recipe, page 51)

Prepare the guacamole ahead of time, cover with plastic wrap placed directly on the mixture to keep the avocados from turning brown and chill while you make the salad.

Mash the avocado with a fork in a medium bowl. Add the garlic, onion, lime juice, cumin, chili powder, salt, pepper, jalapeño pepper and cilantro and mix well.

Brown the ground beef in a large skillet. Add tomatoes, paprika, chili powder and cumin and simmer until meat is cooked through.

Place a large handful of chopped romaine on a plate. Top with a large scoop of ground beef. Sprinkle with diced peppers and top with salsa. Serve with guacamole on the side or right on top. Makes 4 servings.

★ Asian Chicken Salad FRAMPTON FAMILY FAVORITE!

¼ cup tamari

3 tablespoons rice wine vinegar

2 tablespoons coconut crystals

1½ teaspoons dark sesame oil

1½ teaspoons purchased Chili Garlic Sauce (I like Hokan)

3 tablespoons olive oil

1 tablespoon fresh ginger, peeled and grated

2 garlic cloves, minced

1 tablespoon tahini

¾ cup chicken broth

8 cups napa cabbage, shredded (about 1 small head)

1½ cups carrots, grated

5 radishes, sliced (about 1 cup)

½ cup scallions, chopped

3½ cups chicken breasts, cooked and shredded

2 tablespoons sesame seeds, toasted

Combine tamari, vinegar, coconut crystals, sesame oil, and Chili Garlic Sauce in a glass measuring cup. Whisk to blend, then set aside.

Heat olive oil in a small saucepan over medium-high heat. Add ginger and garlic. Cook, stirring, until fragrant, 1 to 2 minutes. Add the tamari mixture to the pan and bring to a simmer. Whisk in tahini and broth. Cook until reduced slightly, 5-10 minutes. Let cool.

Prepare salad, combining cabbage, carrots, radishes, scallions, and chicken in a large bowl. Whisk dressing to recombine and drizzle over the salad. Toss to coat. Sprinkle with sesame seeds. Makes 6 servings.

This is such a great salad. Enjoy it outside on a warm summer afternoon or evening!

Roasted Vegetable Soup

1   large onion, roughly chopped

4   large carrots, peeled and cut into large pieces

6   medium parsnips, peeled and cut into large pieces

1   butternut squash, peeled, seeded and cubed

3   tablespoons olive oil

3   cups chicken broth

½   cup coconut milk

½   teaspoon sea salt

½   teaspoon pepper, or more to taste

Preheat oven to 400 degrees F.

In a large roasting pan combine onion, carrots, parsnips, and squash. Coat well with olive oil and roast, uncovered for 40 minutes, stirring once or twice.

Place roasted vegetables in a large soup pot. Add broth and coconut milk. Season to taste with salt and pepper.

Cook over medium-heat for 20 minutes to allow flavors to combine.

Working in batches, puree the soup in a blender or food processor. (If you have an immersion blender, puree the soup in the soup pot.) Return to the pot and reheat if necessary. Serve warm. Makes 6 servings.

FRAMPTON FAMILY FAVORITE!

This soup freezes beautifully!

Curried Chicken Soup with Coconut

3 tablespoons coconut oil

2 celery stalks, chopped

1 sweet onion, chopped

2 large carrots, chopped

1 large sweet potato, peeled and chopped

1 whole roasted chicken (a purchased rotisserie chicken is a good, easy choice), meat and skin removed and shredded into bite-sized pieces

2 cups chicken broth

1 (14 ounce) can diced tomatoes with their juices

1 (14 ounce) can coconut milk

1-2 teaspoons finely grated lime zest

Juice of 1 lime

1 teaspoon chili paste

1-2 tablespoons curry powder

1 teaspoon turmeric

½ teaspoon cumin

Sea salt and pepper, to taste

This soup is so, so good; there's just nothing else I can say about it!

Freezes well!

In a large soup pot, heat oil over medium heat.

Add celery, onion, carrots and sweet potatoes. Cook uncovered, stirring frequently, for about 20 minutes or until the water from the vegetables have evaporated and the vegetables start to brown.

Add chicken and broth to pot. Add tomatoes, coconut milk, lime zest and lime juice. Mix well.

Add chili paste, turmeric, cumin, curry powder, salt and pepper and stir to blend.

Slowly bring to a boil over medium heat, then cook on low heat and let simmer for 1 hour.

If soup is too thick, add more chicken broth. Makes 6 servings.

Chicken Soup

3	tablespoons olive oil
1	tablespoon ghee (recipe, page 63)
2	large sweet onions, chopped
4	celery stalks, chopped fine
2	large carrots, chopped into little pieces
1	large zucchini, shredded
2	garlic cloves, minced
6	cups chicken broth
2	teaspoons dried basil
½	teaspoon dried oregano
1	teaspoon sea salt
1	teaspoon pepper

Shredded chicken removed from 1 whole roasted or rotisserie chicken

FRAMPTON FAMILY FAVORITE!

Freezes well!

In large soup pot, heat oil and ghee over medium heat.

Add onions, celery, carrots, zucchini and garlic and cook about 20 minutes, stirring frequently, until the water from the vegetables have evaporated and the vegetables turn golden brown. Add a splash of chicken broth if vegetables start to stick or seem to be browning too quickly.

When the vegetables are tender and have turned golden brown, add broth, basil, oregano, salt and pepper and bring to a boil, then reduce heat and simmer uncovered for 15 minutes.

Lower heat, add chicken and simmer 20 minutes longer. Makes 6 servings.

When one of my family members has a cold, this is the soup that's requested!

I shred the zucchini intentionally to thicken the soup and hide it from my girls!

Vegetable Soup

1   tablespoon coconut oil
1   red onion, chopped
2   large leeks, trimmed, well-washed and sliced
3   garlic cloves
4   cups vegetable or chicken broth
1   medium head cauliflower, chopped
1   medium bunch broccoli, chopped
1   teaspoon red chili pepper flakes
⅓   cup coconut milk
Dash of hot sauce, or to taste

Melt the coconut oil in a large soup pot over medium heat. Add the onion and leeks and cook, uncovered, for 15 minutes. Add garlic and cook 5 minutes longer.

Add broth and bring to a boil. Reduce to medium heat.

Add broccoli, cauliflower and chili flakes. Cook over medium heat for about 15 minutes.

Add coconut milk and a dash or two of hot sauce. Simmer 5–10 minutes longer.

Puree with an immersion blender and serve (or puree in batches in a food processor or blender then return to the soup pot to reheat if necessary). Makes 4 servings.

Try adding cooked ground turkey or sausage after puréeing to make this a protein-packed meal.

Roasted Carrot, Parsnip and Ginger Soup

4   large carrots, peeled and chopped
4   parsnips, peeled and chopped
1   onion, sliced
2   garlic cloves, minced
2   tablespoons fresh ginger, grated
6   cups chicken broth, or more, if needed
3   tablespoons olive oil
Sea salt and pepper, to taste

Freezes well!

Preheat oven to 350 degrees F.

Place chopped carrots, parsnips, onions, garlic and 1 tablespoon ginger in a large baking dish and toss with olive oil. Roast uncovered in oven for 15–25 minutes, stirring once, or until the vegetables are tender and deep golden brown.

Add vegetables to a soup pot along with the broth. Bring to a boil and reduce to simmer. Add the other tablespoon of ginger and mix well. Partially cover the pot and cook vegetables about another 10–15 minutes.

Puree with an immersion blender (or puree in batches in a food processor or blender then return the mixture to the soup pot). If the soup is too thick for your taste, add a little more broth to reach desired consistency. Makes 4 servings.

If you want to add a tasty topping, take one extra parsnip and slice (after peeling) with a peeler into large wide strips. Heat ¼ cup (or more) coconut oil in a small skillet over medium-high heat. Season with a little salt and cook until they brown. Remove with slotted spoon to a paper towel to absorb excess oil. Season with a little more salt, and top the soup with crunchy parsnip chips.

Beef Brisket and Sweet Potato Soup

2   tablespoons olive oil

1   sweet onion, chopped

3   celery stalks, chopped

3   carrots, cut into bite-sized pieces

2   teaspoons arrowroot

6   cups chicken broth

2   medium sweet potatoes, peeled and chopped into 1-inch pieces

4   cups beef brisket, chopped from leftover Crock-Pot Brisket (recipe, page 189), shredded into bite-sized pieces

½   teaspoon sea salt (optional)

1   teaspoon pepper

Heat oil in a large soup pot over medium heat. Add onion, celery and carrots and cook about 10 minutes, stirring frequently, until the onions are translucent.

Add arrowroot powder and mix well, stirring constantly making sure there are no lumps. Once the arrowroot is incorporated, add the chicken broth and continue to mix well. Bring to a boil.

Add the sweet potatoes and simmer over low heat for about 20 minutes.

Add the brisket and cook 10 minutes longer over low heat. Add salt and pepper to taste. Serve warm. Makes 6 servings.

This soup is absolutely delicious. I can't say enough good things about the blend of sweet and salty flavors!

Freezes well!

Creamy Broccoli Soup

1   large onion, chopped
2   garlic cloves
1   celery stalk, finely chopped
2   tablespoons olive oil
8   cups broccoli florets
3½ cups chicken broth
1   (14 ounce) can coconut milk
½   teaspoon pepper
½   teaspoon sea salt

In a large soup pot over medium heat, sauté garlic, onion, and celery in olive oil. When the onions are translucent, add broccoli. Sauté a minute more, then add ¼ cup of the chicken broth. Cover and steam for about 10 minutes or until broccoli is tender.

Puree with an immersion blender or, working in batches if necessary, puree in a blender or food processor.

Season with salt and pepper. Add the coconut milk and simmer uncovered for 10–20 minutes longer. Makes 4 servings.

To help you stick to a Paleo lifestyle, don't run out of food! It's worth an extra trip to the farmers' market or grocery store to keep a well-stocked pantry.

Moroccan Chicken Soup

1-2 pounds boneless, skinless chicken breasts, cut into bite-sized pieces
3 tablespoons olive oil
1 tablespoon paprika
2 teaspoons ground cumin
1 teaspoon ground coriander
2 sweet onions, chopped
2 garlic cloves, minced
1 red bell pepper, chopped
1 medium zucchini, chopped
2 medium carrots, peeled and grated
¼ teaspoon cayenne
¼ teaspoon cinnamon
3 tablespoons fresh parsley, finely chopped
6 cups chicken broth
1 cup butternut squash, peeled, seeded and chopped into ½-inch cubes
2 tablespoons lemon juice

Freezes well!

Coat the chicken pieces with 1 tablespoon olive oil. Set aside.

Combine the paprika, cumin and coriander in a small bowl and coat the chicken pieces with the paprika mixture. Set aside.

Heat 1 tablespoon olive oil in a large soup pot on medium heat. Add the chicken and brown on all sides, about 5 minutes. Remove from pot and rest on a plate.

Heat final tablespoon of olive oil and add the onions and garlic to the pot and cook for about 5 minutes. Add the red bell pepper, zucchini and carrot and cook, stirring frequently, for another 10 minutes.

Add cayenne, cinnamon, 2 tablespoons parsley, broth and squash and mix well. Cook 10 minutes longer.

Add the chicken and all the juices that have collected on the plate. Simmer on low for about 10 minutes. Stir in the lemon juice and sprinkle with remaining parsley. Makes 4 servings.

Hearty Butternut Squash Soup

1-2 pounds stew beef, cut into bite-sized pieces

2   tablespoons olive oil or coconut oil

1   sweet onion, diced

2   celery stalks, chopped fine

4   garlic cloves, minced

1   (14 ounce) can diced tomatoes with their juices

6   cups beef broth

2   cups water

1   teaspoon ground cumin

½   butternut squash, peeled, seeded and cut into 1-inch pieces

(you'll have about 3 cups cubed squash)

4   cups kale, chopped

Sea salt and pepper, to garnish

Heat 1 tablespoon of oil in a large skillet over medium heat. Working in batches, add the beef and cook, stirring frequently, about 10 minutes or until browned. When a batch of beef has browned, transfer it to a crock-pot.

Sauté onions, celery, and garlic in a large skillet over medium heat with remaining tablespoon of oil until onions are transparent and are just starting to brown around the edges, about 7 minutes. Add to crock-pot.

Add tomatoes, broth, water, cumin and squash to the crock-pot. Cook on low for 5½ hours.

Add kale, cover and cook 20–30 minutes longer or until kale is tender.

Add salt and pepper and serve hot. Makes 4 servings.

Freezes well!

Pumpkin and Sausage Soup

3 tablespoons ghee (recipe, page 63) or coconut oil, melted

½ medium eggplant, peeled and cut into ½-inch cubes

1 large onion, minced

1-1½ pounds ground breakfast sausage or ground pork sausage

1 (15 ounce) can pumpkin puree

4 cups chicken broth

1 teaspoon dried oregano

1 teaspoon dried thyme

1 tablespoon paprika

¼ teaspoon red pepper flakes

1 teaspoon sea salt or to taste

½ cup coconut milk

Savory and sweet!

Freezes well!

Heat 2 tablespoons of ghee or coconut oil in a soup pot. Sauté the eggplant over medium-high heat until soft and golden, about 15 minutes. Remove the eggplant with a slotted spoon from the pot and place in a small bowl.

Add the remaining ghee or oil to the pot. Add the onion to the pot and sauté over medium heat until golden, about 10–15 minutes.

Add the sausage and brown until it is cooked through. Remove the sausage and onions from the pot and set aside.

Add the pumpkin and broth to the pot and simmer uncovered over medium heat for 10 minutes to deglaze the pot and to blend flavors.

Add the sautéed eggplant. Using an immersion blender, puree the eggplant-pumpkin mixture. Or, puree in a food processor or blender (working in batches if necessary) then return the puree to the pot.

Add the onion and sausage mixture back into the pot and simmer for about 10 minutes.

Add oregano, thyme, paprika, red pepper flakes and salt and simmer uncovered for 20 minutes. Stir in the coconut milk, and let simmer for 5 minutes. Serve hot. Makes 4 servings.

Creamy Tomato Soup

1   tablespoon coconut oil

1   sweet onion, chopped

2   garlic cloves, chopped

2   (28 ounce) cans of diced tomatoes with their juices

1   (16 ounce) can coconut milk or 1½ cups almond milk

1   teaspoon sea salt

½   teaspoon dried basil

Pepper, to taste

In a large soup pot on low-medium heat, sauté the onion in 1 tablespoon of coconut oil until the onions are translucent and start to turn brown, about 10–15 minutes, stirring frequently. Add the garlic and sauté for another 5 minutes. Remove from stove. Let cool 5 minutes.

In a food processor or blender, combine the tomatoes and their juices with the cooked onion and garlic mixture, and blend until smooth. Pour the mixture back into the soup pot. Add the coconut milk, salt, and basil and bring to a boil. Reduce heat and simmer for 10 more minutes. Makes 4 servings.

For a roasted tomato flavor, drain the tomatoes (reserve the juices) and place them in a 9×13 baking dish with a tablespoon of olive oil. Roast for 30 minutes uncovered in a preheated 400 degree oven, stirring occasionally. If the tomatoes seem to be browning too quickly, add some of the reserved tomato juices. Puree the roasted tomatoes and add them to the soup along with reserved tomato juices, just before adding the coconut milk.

Freezes well!

Butternut Squash and Leek Soup

1   whole garlic head
2   tablespoons olive oil
6   cups leeks, trimmed, washed and thinly sliced
1   medium butternut squash, peeled, seeded and cut into 1-inch pieces
1   cup water
3   cups chicken broth
½   teaspoon sea salt
1   teaspoon pepper

Freezes well!

Preheat oven to 350 degrees F.

Remove white papery skin from garlic head (do not peel or separate cloves) and rub the bulb with 1 tablespoon olive oil. Wrap head in foil and bake for 1 hour.

Let cool for 10 minutes. Separate cloves and squeeze to extract garlic pulp into a bowl. Discard skins.

Heat remaining oil in large saucepan over medium-high heat. Add leeks and sauté 10 minutes or until tender. Stir in garlic, butternut squash, water, broth, salt and pepper. Bring to a boil and reduce heat. Simmer for 15 minutes or until squash is tender.

Place half of the squash mixture in a blender. Puree the squash mixture with an immersion blender or use a food processor or blender. If using a blender, remove the center piece of blender lid (to allow steam to escape) and secure the blender lid on the blender. Place a clean towel over the blender lid to avoid splatters and blend until smooth. If using a food processor steam will escape through the feed tube. Repeat with the remaining squash and return the mixture to the saucepan and reheat if necessary. Makes 4 servings.

If you have the energy, make another dinner after you've eaten dinner! Save the second dinner for a feast later in the week.

Gazpacho

4   ripe tomatoes, coarsely chopped

1   small sweet onion, coarsely chopped

1   medium seedless cucumber, peeled and chopped

1   garlic clove

½   cup water

2   tablespoons lemon juice

1   tablespoon drained, prepared horseradish

1   tablespoon fresh parsley, chopped, or 1 teaspoon dried parsley

½   teaspoon pepper

1   cup crushed ice

Blend all ingredients in a food processor until all vegetables are finely chopped or pureed; choosing whichever consistency you prefer.

Serve. Makes 2 servings.

Fresh, cool, and perfect for a warm summer day!

Freezes well!

Vegetables and Sides

Ah, so many vegetables to choose from! Remember that any vegetable side dish is perfect for rounding out a Paleo meal. There are several "side" recipes offered in this chapter. Even though simple steamed, roasted or grilled vegetables taste terrific, don't be shy about getting creative: add herbs, spices, citrus juices, zests and oils.

Roasting

Roasting adds great flavor and natural sweetness to so many vegetables. Take any of the vegetables listed below by themselves or in combination and chop to bite size or any size you want and combine with 2 tablespoons melted coconut oil or ghee, sea salt and ground pepper. Mix thoroughly and place on a large baking dish. Roast at 400 degrees for about 10–30 minutes or until crisp-tender.

Broccoli, cauliflower, beets, butternut squash and other winter squashes, asparagus, Brussels sprouts, zucchini, peppers, onions, turnips, parsnips, leeks, fennel, cabbage, sweet potatoes and eggplant.

Get brave! Add spices and herbs to give your vegetables a flavorful Asian, Mexican or Italian kick. Have fun; raid your spice cabinet and snip herbs from the garden. See page 15 for spice and herb suggestions.

Onions and peppers all week:

Every Sunday evening I thinly slice 8 sweet onions and 4-6 red peppers. I mix with some olive oil (you can also use coconut oil or ghee), sea salt, and pepper, divide them into two large glass baking dishes, and place them in the oven at 300 degrees F for about 1-2 hours. Then, I place them in containers in the refrigerator and use them throughout the week as add-ins to breakfast, lunch, and dinner recipes. They're also great reheated and served as a side or by themselves. So easy and delicious!

Steaming & Blanching

Steam any of your favorite vegetables in a steaming basket until crisp-tender. Or, blanch them in a pot of boiling water for just a few minutes. Be careful not to overcook. Choices abound! Visit your local green market and choose farm-fresh vegetables such as broccoli, cauliflower, zucchini, summer squash, Brussels sprouts, asparagus and even green beans (yes, I know "they're not Paleo").

Grilling

Slice and grill any vegetable—especially during the summer. There are so many fresh varieties to choose from. To grill, rinse vegetables, cut or trim as desired, then coat with olive oil or melted coconut oil. Sprinkle with sea salt and pepper plus any other spices and herbs that you're craving. Grill the veggies until crisp-tender or to desired texture.

Grow your own vegetables and herbs if you can; it'll make you happy, proud, and keep you well fed!

Sautéing

Cooking vegetables in a skillet—uncovered—with a bit of olive oil or coconut oil is both quick and easy. Almost any vegetable can be sautéed. (Timing will depend on the type of vegetable.) Add herbs, spices, sea salt and pepper. Sautéing is especially great for greens like chard, spinach and kale.

Mashing

Nearly everyone likes mashed potatoes, but there are so many other vegetables that can be cooked and mashed. Roast, steam, blanch or boil vegetables until soft then mash them in a bowl with a bit of coconut milk or ghee. Add sea salt and pepper plus spices and herbs (or even minced chipotle in adobe sauce) to taste. Try combining more than one vegetable to make a "mash;" have fun and be creative.

Spaghetti Squash with Lemon and Asparagus

1	medium spaghetti squash
2	tablespoons olive oil
2	tablespoons shallots, minced
2	scallions, chopped
2	garlic cloves, minced
½	cup chicken broth
½	teaspoon dried marjoram
1	teaspoon grated lemon zest
½	teaspoon sea salt
12	asparagus spears, trimmed and cut into 2-inch pieces
2	tablespoons fresh lemon juice

Preheat oven to 350 degrees F.

Cut squash in half, length wise. Scoop out seeds. Place squash in baking dish, cut side down, with about ½ inch water. Bake about 45 minutes, until tender.

While squash is cooking, heat oil in a large skillet over medium heat. Add shallots, scallions and garlic and sauté for a couple of minutes or until slightly softened.

Remove squash from oven and let stand at room temperature until cool enough to handle. In a medium bowl, separate squash flesh with a fork to form spaghetti-like strands. Set aside.

Add broth, marjoram, lemon zest and salt to the skillet. Bring to a boil, then add asparagus.

Reduce heat and simmer, covered, for about 2 minutes.

Stir the asparagus mixture into the bowl of spaghetti squash. Add fresh lemon juice to taste. Mix well. Makes 6 servings.

FRAMPTON FAMILY FAVORITE!

Nutty Butternut Squash with Vanilla

1   medium butternut squash, peeled, seeded and cut into 1-inch cubes

4   tablespoons coconut oil, melted

1½ cups of walnuts, toasted

2   teaspoons ground ginger

2   teaspoons vanilla extract

Pepper to taste

¼   teaspoon sea salt

Juice of ½ lemon

Preheat oven to 400 degrees F.

Place squash with 2 tablespoons of the coconut oil in a large baking dish and toss lightly to blend. Sprinkle with salt and bake for 20 minutes or until tender and squash is beginning to brown around the edges. Remove from oven.

Heat a large skillet over medium-high heat and toast the walnuts for 3–5 minutes or until they are lightly browned. Nuts burn easily, so watch them carefully.

Add 2 tablespoons of coconut oil to the skillet with the walnuts over medium-high heat. Toss the walnuts to coat with coconut oil then add the squash and mix well.

Add the ginger, vanilla extract, pepper and salt to taste. Mix everything together gently. Remove from heat and squeeze lemon juice over mixture. Serve hot. Makes 4 servings.

If you like spicy food, use spices liberally for a burst of flavor. If you have fresh herbs, use them; if not, dried herbs are fine.

Paleo "Stuffing"

½   pound extra-lean ground beef
1   pound ground pork sausage
1   large sweet onion, diced
4   celery stalks, diced
2   apples, peeled and finely diced (choose a sweet variety)
1   cup golden raisins
¼   teaspoon dried rosemary
¼   teaspoon dried sage
¼   teaspoon dried thyme
¼   teaspoon dried marjoram
1   teaspoon garlic powder
2   cups walnuts, (these need to be soaked in water overnight, rinsed
and finely chopped before using the next day)
½   teaspoon sea salt

Preheat the oven to 375 degrees F.

Sauté the beef and pork in a heated pot for 2–3 minutes on medium heat, making sure that the meat gets broken up into small pieces as it cooks. Be careful not to brown the meat; you should still see some pink. The meat will cook fully in the oven.

Add the onion, celery, raisins and apples, and cook for another 5 minutes.

Add the spices, garlic powder, walnuts and salt, and mix thoroughly. Pour everything from the pan, into a greased 9×13 baking dish, and bake for 30–40 minutes. Serve immediately. Makes 6 servings.

FRAMPTON FAMILY FAVORITE!

Losing the bread from any stuffing recipe may sound too radical, but this tastes great and the texture is as "stuffing like" as you can get without the bread!

Roasted Carrots and Onions

2 cups baby carrots
2 sweet onions, quartered
2 tablespoons olive oil
2 tablespoons balsamic vinegar
2 tablespoons raw honey

Preheat oven to 325 degrees F.

In a bowl whisk together olive oil, vinegar and honey. Put vegetables into the bowl and mix to coat. Remove vegetables from bowl and place evenly on greased baking sheet. Pour remaining mixture over the vegetables.

Bake for about 40 minutes or until vegetables are tender, stirring once during cooking time. Makes 4 servings.

Spicy Lemon Cauliflower

1 head of cauliflower, separated into florets
2 tablespoons olive oil
1 tablespoon of lemon zest
2 tablespoons of lemon juice
1 teaspoon red pepper flakes

Preheat oven to 400 degrees F.

Combine all ingredients in a bowl and mix thoroughly to coat all of the cauliflower. Pour mixture onto baking sheet and bake for about 20 minutes. Stir the cauliflower once during this time. You want a little browning on the edges of the cauliflower. Serve. Makes 4 servings.

You can substitute lime juice and cilantro and turned this into a Mexican side dish!

Sweet Potato Hash

2 tablespoons coconut oil

1 medium onion, chopped

½ cup red bell pepper, finely chopped

1 medium sweet potato, peeled and diced into ½-inch cubes

1-2 tablespoons vegetable or chicken broth

Sea salt and pepper

Heat the oil in a skillet over medium heat.

Add onions and peppers and sauté for 10 minutes. Look for soft onions that are beginning to brown.

Add the sweet potatoes and 1 tablespoon of broth.

Cover and cook for 15 minutes or until the potatoes are soft, stirring frequently to keep them from burning. Add a bit more broth if needed (you want the potatoes to brown so be careful not to add too much broth, as the potatoes will turn to mush).

Serve with salt and pepper. Makes 2 servings.

This hash is fabulous! Double the recipe and enjoy it for breakfast the following day. Delicious!

Vegetable Latkes

3 cups grated vegetables (try using a combination of three: carrots, turnips, daikon radishes, zucchini, sweet potatoes or summer squash)

1 cup grated sweet onion

2 eggs, beaten

1 teaspoon sea salt and pepper

½ cup (or more) coconut oil for frying

Preheat oven to 250 degrees F.

Wrap a dish towel or several paper towels around 1 cup of grated vegetable/onion mixture at a time and squeeze as much water out as possible.

In a bowl, mix grated vegetables with eggs, salt and pepper.

Heat ½ cup coconut oil over medium to medium-high heat. Make sure oil is hot before cooking latkes. Scoop ¼ cup of grated vegetables into your hand and form a loose latke/patty. Set the latke in the hot pan and press it down gently with a fork. Working in batches, place 3 or 4 latkes in the pan at a time.

Cook at least 2–3 minutes on each side, until browned.

Transfer to a baking sheet and keep warm inside oven while you cook the remaining latkes.

If the oil becomes dark, discard it. Wipe out the skillet with paper towels and add additional oil as needed to finish cooking the latkes.

Serve as is or with some unsweetened apple sauce. Makes 4 servings.

Hydration is important to digestion. Drink one to two glasses of water before each meal.

Roasted Brussels Sprouts with Bacon

3　tablespoons olive oil

½　pound bacon, chopped

3　shallots, sliced thin

1　pound Brussels sprouts, trimmed and halved

1　tablespoon ghee (recipe, page 63), melted

Juice of 1 lemon

Sea salt and pepper to taste

Preheat oven to 375 degrees F.

Heat oil over medium-high heat in a large skillet. Add bacon and cook until crisp. Remove bacon from the pan and set bacon aside on paper towels to drain excess fat.

Add shallots to the pan and cook for 2–3 minutes until soft. Add Brussels sprouts and toss to combine.

Spread Brussels sprout mixture onto a baking sheet. Season with desired salt and pepper and then roast in the oven until vegetables are cooked and golden brown, about 10–15 minutes.

Remove from the oven. Stir in ghee and lemon juice and mix well. Move to a serving dish and top with bacon. Makes 4 servings.

Add some toasted pine nuts and raisins to give this side some sweet crunch.

Butternut Squash with Cranberries

2   cups butternut squash, peeled, seeded and diced into ½-inch cubes

2   tablespoons coconut oil, melted

½   onion, diced

¼   cup dried cranberries

¼   cup vegetable or chicken broth

1   teaspoon curry powder

1   teaspoon cardamom

Preheat oven to 425 degrees F.

Place squash in a medium baking dish and toss with 1 tablespoon of coconut oil. Bake for 15 minutes or until tender but not mushy.

In a medium skillet over medium-high heat, sauté the onion in the other tablespoon of coconut oil for about 10 minutes or until the onion is translucent and beginning to brown around the edges.

Take squash out of oven and add to onion. Mix well.

Add the cranberries, broth, curry powder and cardamom. Stir until warmed through. Makes 4 servings.

Paleo on a budget: Yes! It can be done. Buy inexpensive cuts of meat and braise them or roast slowly in the oven with broth until tender. Buy vegetables in season or purchase frozen vegetables when they're on sale.

Roasted Brussels Sprouts

1   pound Brussels sprouts, outside leaves removed and stems trimmed
6   bacon strips, cooked and chopped
1   tablespoon dried dill weed or basil
Olive oil to taste
Pepper to taste

Preheat oven to 350 degrees F.

Steam Brussels sprouts for 4 minutes. Cool until easy to handle then slice into quarters. Mix in a bowl with bacon, dillweed, olive oil and pepper and toss to blend. Spread evenly in a 9×13 glass baking dish and bake for 30 minutes or until Brussels sprouts are tender but not mushy. Stir once half way through cooking time, and serve hot. Makes 4 servings.

Curried Cauliflower

1   medium head of cauliflower
½   cup olive oil
2   teaspoons curry powder
1   tablespoon garlic powder
½   teaspoon turmeric
1   teaspoon chili powder
¼   teaspoon sea salt

This is so delicious; we make it frequently!

Preheat oven to 350 degrees F.

Pour about ½ cup of olive oil into a large bowl. Add curry powder, garlic powder, turmeric, chili powder and salt. Mix well. Break up the head of cauliflower (use mostly the flowers, not the stems) and add to the bowl of olive oil mixture. Mix until the cauliflower is fully coated with the oil mixture, spread evenly on a baking sheet and bake for 40–45 minutes or until tender but not mushy. Stir at least once halfway through cooking. Serve hot or warm. Makes 4 servings.

Cauliflower "Fried Rice"

1   head cauliflower, chopped and steamed
1   red onion, minced
3   garlic cloves, minced
½   cup carrots, grated
1   tablespoon dried basil
1   egg, beaten
2   tablespoons coconut flour
1   teaspoon sea salt and pepper to taste
3-4 tablespoons coconut oil

In a large bowl, add the onion, garlic, carrots, and basil.

Place the cauliflower in the bowl and add the egg, coconut flour, salt and pepper.

Using a potato masher or fork, mash the cauliflower down to the consistency of rice. Mix all the ingredients well.

Heat coconut oil in a large skillet over medium-high heat. Add the cauliflower "rice" mixture and sauté for 10–15 minutes or until the "rice" starts to crisp up a little. The crispy part is important, so be patient. Makes 4 servings.

Note: For simple Cauliflower "Rice," just steam cauliflower florets and mash with a fork or potato masher to the consistency of rice; add sea salt and pepper to taste. Add a little ghee or coconut oil for more flavor.

VEGETABLES AND SIDES

Spanish-Style Cauliflower "Rice"

1   head cauliflower, chopped
1   tablespoon olive oil
3   garlic cloves, minced
1   onion, finely chopped
1   small red bell pepper, finely chopped
1   (4 ounce) can diced green chilies
2   tablespoons tomato paste
1   tablespoon water
Sea salt and pepper to taste, optional
3   tablespoons fresh cilantro, leaves removed and chopped

Pulse the cauliflower in a food processor to create the "rice" consistency. Set aside.

Heat olive oil in a skillet, and sauté onion, garlic, and bell pepper for about 10–15 minutes or until onion is translucent and beginning to brown. Add tomato paste, green chilies and water.

Turn heat down to low and add chopped cauliflower. Add salt and pepper. Mix well and cook uncovered for another 10 minutes or until the liquids have evaporated and the "rice" has browned a bit.

Transfer to a serving dish if desired, top with cilantro and serve hot or warm. Makes 4 servings.

Broccoli with Caramelized Onions and Pine Nuts

1   tablespoon olive oil
1   onion, chopped
3   tablespoons pine nuts
4   cups broccoli florets
2   teaspoons balsamic vinegar
Sea salt and pepper to taste

Warm the olive oil in a large skillet over medium heat. Add the onion, salt and pepper to taste. Cook about 10 minutes or until onion is tender. Set aside.

Toast the pine nuts in a dry skillet over medium-low heat for 2–3 minutes, stirring constantly; do not burn. Remove from heat and let cool.

Steam broccoli until just tender (or to desired consistency). Put broccoli in large bowl and add onion, pine nuts and vinegar. Mix well. Add a little more olive oil and/or salt and pepper to taste. Makes 4 servings.

Tangy Cole Slaw

1   cup purple cabbage, shredded
1   cup green cabbage, shredded
½   cup carrots, shredded
¼   cup sweet onion, finely chopped
Lemon juice from one whole lemon
2   tablespoons apple cider vinegar
6   tablespoons olive oil
1   tablespoon Dijon mustard
1   teaspoon celery seed
Pepper to taste

If you want a little more kick to your coleslaw, add a teaspoon of chipotle pepper seasoning.

Mix all ingredients in a large bowl. Add spices to desired flavor. Mix well and serve. Makes 4 servings.

Poultry

One of the secrets to any good chicken recipe is to not overcook the chicken. Remember, when grilling, frying, baking or broiling chicken, less is more. It's better to cook the chicken until a meat thermometer registers 160 degrees F; remove the chicken from the heat and cover before serving. The chicken will continue to cook as it rests. Do not overcook or chicken might be tough and dry. Ideally, chicken should be tender enough to cut with a fork or butter knife. When using a slow cooker or Dutch oven, long, slow cooking nearly always guarantees tender, melt-in-the mouth chicken.

Chicken Tenders with Peppers and Onions

½ teaspoon freshly grated lemon zest

3 tablespoons lemon juice

2 tablespoons garlic, minced

1 teaspoon dried oregano

2 jalapeño peppers, seeded and finely chopped

2 tablespoons olive oil

½ teaspoon sea salt

1 pound chicken tenders

1 red, yellow, or orange bell pepper, seeded and thinly sliced

1 medium onion, thinly sliced

Preheat oven to 425 degrees F.

Whisk together lemon zest, lemon juice, garlic, oregano, jalapeños, oil and salt in a large bowl. Pour into a 9×3 inch glass baking dish.

Add chicken, bell peppers, and onions. Toss to coat.

Spread the mixture out evenly. Cover with foil. Bake until the chicken is cooked through, about 15 minutes or until a meat thermometer registers 160 degrees when placed in the thickest chicken tender. Makes 4 servings.

FRAMPTON FAMILY FAVORITE!

Substitute sausage links instead of chicken for an Italian flavor, or combine the two.

Salsa Chicken

2   tablespoons coconut oil

1 to 2 pounds boneless, skinless chicken thighs

1 to 2 pounds boneless, skinless chicken breasts

Sea salt and pepper to taste

1   sweet onion, chopped

1   (28 ounce) can of organic diced tomatoes

1   (12 ounce) jar of salsa verde, preferably Trader Joe's

1   mango, peeled and diced

1   tablespoon chili powder

1   tablespoon paprika

*Salsa Chicken
freezes beautifully!*

Preheat oven to 350 degrees F.

In a Dutch oven, heat coconut oil over medium heat. Place chicken in the Dutch oven and sprinkle with salt and pepper. Brown the chicken for about 3–5 minutes per side, turning occasionally. Remove the chicken and set aside.

Add the onions and sauté for about 10 minutes. Add the diced tomatoes, salsa verde, mango, chili powder, paprika and some pepper. Mix well. Let simmer a few minutes.

Place the chicken back into the Dutch oven and mix with the sauce. Place covered Dutch oven into oven and cook for 2 hours. Serve hot. Use fork to pull apart the chicken if you wish, before serving. Makes 8 servings.

FRAMPTON FAMILY FAVORITE!

*This is terrific over Cauliflower "Rice"
(see note, recipe, page 113).*

Turkey and Veggie Burgers

1½ pounds ground turkey breast

1   medium zucchini, grated

1   medium carrot, grated

3   garlic cloves, minced

1   egg

2   tablespoons fresh or 1½ teaspoons dried thyme

¾   teaspoon sea salt

1   teaspoon pepper

2   tablespoons coconut oil, melted

Preheat broiler or grill to medium-high.

Wrap zucchini in several layers of paper towels to absorb excess moisture.

Combine the turkey, zucchini, carrot, garlic, egg, thyme, salt and pepper in a large bowl and mix to blend. Form the mixture into ½-inch thick patties.

Brush with the coconut oil and grill or broil the burgers 4–5 minutes per side or longer, if desired.

Makes about six burgers.

FRAMPTON FAMILY FAVORITE!

Don't be afraid to try other spices. Mix in one chopped chipotle pepper in adobe sauce for a spicy/smoky flavor.

Pecan-Crusted Chicken

4   boneless, skinless chicken breasts
½   cup organic spicy brown or Dijon mustard
3   tablespoons raw honey
1   cup pecans
Sea salt, to taste
Coconut oil

Preheat oven to 350 degrees F.

Whisk together the honey and mustard in a medium-sized bowl.

Toss the pecans in a food processor and pulse until the nuts are finely chopped. Pour the chopped pecans on a plate.

Use a paper towel to pat the chicken breasts dry. Taking one chicken breast at a time, place the chicken into the honey mustard mixture and coat on both sides. Roll chicken in chopped pecans.

Place coated chicken into a greased glass baking dish. Sprinkle each chicken breast with salt.

Bake for 25–35 minutes or until a meat thermometer inserted in the thickest part reads 160 degrees F. Makes 4 servings.

This simple, delicious dish can be made with other nuts, too. Try almonds, hazelnuts, cashews or macadamia nuts.

Easy Appetizer: Cut the cooked chicken into bite-sized pieces and serve warm with toothpicks.

Dijon Chicken Stew

4	tablespoons olive oil
3	leeks, washed and chopped
4	garlic cloves, minced
½	teaspoon sea salt
½	teaspoon pepper
2	pounds boneless, skinless chicken thighs and breasts, cut into 1-inch cubes
1	cup dry white wine
3	cups chicken broth
1	tablespoon arrowroot
1½	cups water
2	tablespoons Dijon mustard
2	medium sweet potatoes, peeled and cubed
6	cups kale leaves, torn

Crushed red pepper flakes, to taste

Freezes well.

Heat 1 tablespoon of oil in a Dutch oven over medium-high heat. Add the leeks and sauté for about 5 minutes. Add the garlic and sauté another minute. Spoon mixture out of pot and into bowl, and set aside.

Season the chicken with salt and pepper. Place another tablespoon of oil in Dutch oven and add chicken pieces. Brown all sides.

Remove chicken and add it to the leek mixture.

Add wine to the Dutch oven, scraping the loose bits.

Combine 1 cup of broth with arrowroot in a small bowl and whisk thoroughly. Add to the pot along with remaining 2 cups of broth, water, and mustard. Bring to a boil.

Add chicken and leeks to the pot. Cover and simmer over low heat for about 20 minutes. Add sweet potatoes and simmer 20 more minutes or until potatoes are tender but not mushy.

Add kale and simmer 10 more minutes or until kale is tender. Do not overcook. Enjoy with a dash of red pepper flakes. Makes 6 servings.

Crock-Pot Chicken Chili

2 pounds ground chicken

3 tablespoons chili powder

2 (28 ounce) cans of diced tomatoes with juice

1 large sweet potato, peeled and shredded

2 cups chicken broth

2 chipotle chilies in adobe sauce, chopped

2 tablespoons tamari

1 teaspoon sea salt

1 tablespoon garlic powder

1 tablespoon onion powder

1 teaspoon dried oregano

1 teaspoon ground cumin

¼ teaspoon cinnamon

Place ground chicken in the crock-pot. Add chili powder, tomatoes and their juices, sweet potato, chicken broth, chipotle chilies, tamari, salt and spices. Stir everything together and mix well.

Cover and cook on low for 6–8 hours. Makes 6 servings.

Freezes well.

Make healthy food purchases as often as you can.

Thai Chicken Wraps

12 bibb or romaine lettuce leaves

4 napa cabbage leaves, thinly chopped

1 pound chicken breast, grilled (or use chicken from rotisserie bird) and then diced into ½ inch cubes

1 cup raw broccoli, finely chopped

½ cup carrots, grated

½ cup scallions, thinly sliced

Thai Sauce:

¼ cup almond butter

¼ cup water

2 tablespoons tamari

2 tablespoons lime juice

2 garlic cloves, minced

Combine almond butter, water, tamari, lime juice and garlic in a medium bowl and whisk to blend.

Spread out the lettuce leaves on a flat surface. Place a tablespoon of napa cabbage in the center of each leaf. Add 1 tablespoon of each of chicken, broccoli, carrots and scallions on top of the cabbage. Drizzle with Thai Sauce and serve immediately. Makes 4 servings.

Zucchini can be substituted for the broccoli; it's great!

Spicy Crock-Pot Chicken

1   onion, sliced
1   teaspoon sea salt
2   tablespoons paprika
1   teaspoon cayenne
1   teaspoon pepper
2   teaspoons garlic powder
1   5-6 pound whole chicken, patted dry with paper towels
1   lemon, cut in half

Cover the bottom of the crock pot with the onion.

Mix salt, paprika, cayenne, pepper and garlic powder in a small bowl and then rub the spice mixture over the whole chicken. Place lemon halves in cavity of the chicken.

Place the chicken on top of the onion in the crock-pot, cover, and cook on low for 5–6 hours.

Remove from crock-pot and use a fork to remove meat from bones. Discard bones and lemon.

Spoon the onion and a little bit of the juices over the chicken when you serve. Makes 4 servings.

One reason I love this recipe is because the chicken falls right of the bones. I like the balance of spices here, but feel free to adjust them to your liking.

Ground Turkey and Squash Casserole

1-2 pounds ground turkey (you could also use ground beef)
1   butternut squash, peeled, seeded and diced
1   medium sweet onion, chopped
2   tablespoons chili powder
2   tablespoons balsamic vinegar
2   teaspoons garlic powder
1   teaspoon pepper
1   teaspoon sea salt
2   tablespoons olive oil

Preheat oven to 350 degrees F.

Add turkey, squash, onion, chili powder, 1 tablespoon vinegar, garlic powder, salt, pepper and olive oil to a mixing bowl. Mix all ingredients thoroughly and then transfer to a 9×13 baking dish.

Splash the other tablespoon balsamic vinegar over the top.

Cook covered for 60 minutes or until squash is tender but not mushy and the turkey is thoroughly cooked but not dry. Makes 6 servings.

Easy! For a spicier dish, add cayenne or ground chipotle pepper seasoning.

Bonus: leftovers are great with fried eggs the next day.

Green Chili Turkey Burgers

1   pound ground turkey breast

1   (6-ounce) can diced green chilies (do not drain)

½   cup fresh cilantro, leaves removed and finely chopped

½   cup onion, finely chopped

2   teaspoons cumin

1   tablespoon chili powder

2   teaspoons paprika

2   teaspoons coriander

1   teaspoon sea salt

Preheat a grill to medium.

Mix turkey, chilies and their juices, cilantro, onion, cumin, chili powder, paprika, coriander and salt in a medium bowl. Mix to blend.

Form into burgers and grill 4–6 minutes per side or to desired degree of doneness. Makes approximately 4 burgers.

FRAMPTON FAMILY FAVORITE!

Top with a fried egg for an amazing dinner or breakfast. Serve with Sweet Potato Chips (page 51) or Sweet Potato Hash (page 108), if desired for a Paleo version of "burgers and fries!"

Chicken with Sun Dried Tomatoes and Artichoke Hearts

3   pounds boneless, skinless chicken breasts or thighs,
cut into 1- to 2-inch pieces.

3-4 tablespoons olive oil

2   tablespoons paprika

1   teaspoon sea salt

1   large sweet onion, chopped

1   (7 ounce) jar sun dried tomatoes packed in oil, drained and chopped

1   (12 ounce) jar marinated artichoke hearts, drained and chopped

3   cups chicken broth

1   tablespoon dried oregano

Sea salt and pepper, to taste

Preheat oven to 350 degrees F.

Place the chicken pieces in a large bowl and toss with 1 tablespoon of olive oil, paprika and salt.

Heat Dutch oven over high heat. Add 2 tablespoons olive oil and sear chicken pieces on all sides until browned, 2–3 minutes. Work in batches if necessary.

Remove chicken from Dutch oven and set aside.

In the same Dutch oven, add another tablespoon of olive oil (if needed) and add onion. Sauté for about 10 minutes.

Add sun dried tomatoes and artichoke hearts and cook another minute or two.

Add broth, oregano, salt, and pepper and simmer for 10 minutes.

Add chicken pieces to the Dutch oven. Mix well. Cover and place in oven to cook for about another hour, stirring once during cooking time. Makes 6 servings.

✪ Chicken and Sausage Cacciatore

2 tablespoons coconut oil

4-6 boneless, skinless chicken breasts

2 onions, sliced into thin strips

2 bell peppers, sliced into thin strips

1 pound ground pork sausage

1 (28 ounce) can crushed tomatoes in puree

1 cup chicken broth

½ cup dry red wine

1 tablespoon Italian seasoning

1 teaspoon pepper

1 teaspoon sea salt

FRAMPTON FAMILY FAVORITE!

Freezes well.

Preheat oven to 350 degrees F.

Heat coconut oil in Dutch oven over medium-high heat, and sear chicken breast on both sides for about 3 minutes. Remove chicken from pot. Set aside.

Add onions and peppers to the pot and cook 15 minutes until they are cooked and starting to brown. Add the sausage and cook for 5 minutes until it begins to brown. Add tomato puree, chicken broth, red wine, Italian seasoning, pepper and salt. Simmer about 10–15 minutes.

Add chicken breast back to the pot. Place in oven for 1–2 hours. Stir a couple of times and remove when sauce has reached desired thickness.

Shred chicken using a fork. Serve alone or with spaghetti squash on the side. Makes 6 servings.

You can make this recipe in a crock-pot as well by adding all ingredients in the pot and cooking on low for 6-7 hours. I would still recommend searing the chicken and sautéing the onions, peppers and sausage before adding to the crock-pot; it adds great flavor.

POULTRY

Easy Chicken BLT

½ cup organic mayonnaise (Basic Mayonnaise recipe, page 67)
½ cup cilantro, leaves removed and finely chopped
Juice from 1 lime
Cooked chicken, shredded by hand (use leftover chicken or purchased rotisserie chicken)
1 pound bacon, cooked and drained
Romaine lettuce hearts, leaves separated
Tomatoes, sliced or chopped

Mix mayonnaise with cilantro and lime juice in a medium bowl. Set aside.

Layer each romaine lettuce leaf with teaspoon or more of cilantro-lime mayonnaise, piece of bacon, some tomato and some chicken. Fold over (as you would a soft tortilla) and serve at room temperature. Makes 4 servings.

FRAMPTON FAMILY FAVORITE!

These are so easy and delicious. We eat them as snacks as well as a meal.

Chicken Piccata

4   boneless, skinless chicken breasts
2   tablespoons coconut oil
Sea salt and pepper, to taste
3   tablespoons olive oil
6   garlic cloves, minced
1   sweet onion, finely diced
¼   cup dry white wine
½   cup chicken broth
Juice and zest from 1 lemon
2   tablespoons capers, drained

I love lemon, so I often add extra!

Place the chicken pieces between 2 pieces of parchment paper. With the flat side of a meat mallet, gently pound the chicken until it's approximately ½ inch thick.

In a large skillet, heat the coconut oil over medium-high heat. While the pan is heating, sprinkle both sides of the chicken with salt and pepper. Place the chicken into the skillet and cook on both sides for 2 minutes. Remove the chicken from the skillet.

Add olive oil, garlic and onion to skillet and sauté for about 10 minutes, scraping the chicken drippings off the bottom of the skillet.

Add the wine, chicken broth, lemon juice, lemon zest and capers. Bring to a simmer for 2–5 minutes.

Add chicken breast back in the skillet. Cover and simmer over low heat for 2–3 minutes. Makes 4 servings.

FRAMPTON FAMILY FAVORITE!

This is great over Cauliflower "Rice" (see note, recipe, page 113) because the cauliflower absorbs the tasty juices. So good!

Mustard-Lime Chicken

½ cup fresh lime juice

½ cup fresh cilantro, leaves removed and finely chopped

¼ cup Dijon mustard

1 tablespoon olive oil

1 tablespoon chili powder

½ teaspoon sea salt

½ teaspoon pepper

4 boneless, skinless chicken breasts

Preheat grill to medium-high.

Combine lime juice, cilantro, mustard, olive oil, chili powder, salt and pepper in a food processor and pulse until well combined.

Place chicken breasts in glass baking dish or plastic Ziploc bag. Pour marinade over chicken, cover and refrigerate for at least 30 minutes or up to 6 hours.

Cook chicken for 5 minutes per side until browned and cooked in the center. Makes 4 servings.

Love this recipe; great flavor! The chicken is terrific to have on hand (I like to make it on Sundays) for protein snacks throughout the week.

You can substitute lemon juice for lime juice and basil for cilantro and have another great-tasting marinade.

Chicken with Cilantro-Lime Pesto

4   boneless, skinless chicken breasts, cut into 1-inch cubes

Sea salt and pepper, to taste

1   tablespoon coconut oil

Cilantro-Lime Pesto

1   jalapeño pepper, seeded and chopped

1   tablespoon ginger paste or powder

2   garlic cloves

¼   cup coconut milk

1   large bunch of cilantro, chopped

½   teaspoon of sea salt

Juice of 2 limes

Season chicken with salt and pepper.

Heat coconut oil in a skillet over medium-high heat. Add chicken and sauté until cooked through. Remove from skillet and cool.

In food processor, puree jalapeño pepper, garlic, ginger and coconut milk until it is smooth and thick. Add cilantro. Pulse until blended. Add salt. With food processor running add lime juice slowly.

Remove from food processor and serve over the chicken. Makes 4 servings.

The pesto will keep refrigerated for up to a month or you can freeze it—if there's any left over!

This dish can also be a great little appetizer; just serve with toothpicks.

Chicken Saltimbocca

Chicken

4 boneless, skinless chicken breasts

2 tablespoons dried sage

½ pound prosciutto, thinly sliced

2 tablespoons ghee (recipe, page 63)

Sauce

2 shallots, thinly sliced

1 tablespoon ghee

⅓ cup dry white wine

¼ cup chicken broth

1 teaspoon arrowroot, dissolved in 2 tablespoons cold water

Working with one chicken breast at a time, lay the breast flat on a cutting board and use a very sharp knife to cut through the breasts horizontally in order to create 2 thinner slices of chicken. Spread the slices out on a flat surface.

Place a pinch of dried sage on the chicken. Place a slice of prosciutto on top of the sage and pat it gently so that it sticks to the chicken.

Heat 2 tablespoons ghee in a large skillet over medium-high heat. Working in batches if necessary (don't crowd the skillet), place the chicken in the skillet prosciutto-side-up and cook until browned on the bottom, about 2–3 minutes. Flip each piece over so that each piece is prosciutto-side-down. Cook about 2–3 minutes or until prosciutto is slightly crispy and chicken is cooked through.

As each piece is done, transfer to a platter and cover to keep warm. Continue with the remaining chicken, adding additional ghee if necessary.

Once all of the chicken is cooked, add 1 tablespoon ghee and shallots to the pan and sauté for 5–10 minutes. Add wine and broth. Once the liquid has reduced a bit, stir in the arrowroot and cold water mixture. Stir quickly to thicken. Pour the sauce over the chicken and serve immediately. Makes 4–6 servings.

Butter Chicken

4   tablespoons ghee (recipe, page 63)

2½ pounds boneless, skinless chicken breast, cut into bite-sized pieces

1   red onion, finely diced

2   teaspoons cardamom

2   teaspoons coriander

1   teaspoon fenugreek powder

2   teaspoons garam masala

½   teaspoon chili powder

1   teaspoon paprika

1   teaspoon sea salt

1   (8 ounce) can tomato puree

¾   cup coconut milk

Juice of ½ lemon

Heat 2 tablespoons of the ghee in a large, heavy skillet over medium heat. Add the chicken and stir-fry until cooked through but not tough. Transfer the chicken to a plate and set aside.

Add 2 more tablespoons of ghee to pan. Add onion and cook for 5 minutes, until soft. Add cardamom, coriander, fenugreek, garam masala, chili powder, paprika and salt. Cook, stirring frequently, 1–2 minutes or until the spices release their fragrance.

Put the chicken back in the skillet and mix in all the spices with the chicken.

Add the tomato puree and simmer for about 15 minutes, stirring from time to time. Add the coconut milk and lemon juice and let it simmer another 5 minutes. Makes 4 servings.

When you simplify dinner to meat, vegetables and healthy fats, cooking is EASY!

Crock-Pot Chicken Stew

4   carrots, peeled and cut into bite-sized pieces

4   celery stalks, finely chopped

½   pound white mushrooms, cleaned and quartered

½   pound cremini mushrooms, cleaned and quartered

1   onion, roughly chopped

6   garlic cloves, minced

1   teaspoon dried rosemary

1   teaspoon dried parsley

½   teaspoon dried basil

½   teaspoon dried sage

1   teaspoon sea salt, or more to taste

1   teaspoon pepper, or more to taste

2   tablespoons tomato paste

¼   cup organic chicken broth

1   (28 ounce) can diced tomatoes with their juices

1   pound boneless, skinless chicken thighs

2   pounds boneless, skinless chicken breasts

2   small bay leaves

Place carrots, celery, mushrooms, onion, garlic, rosemary, parsley, basil, sage, salt and pepper in crock-pot and mix to combine. Dissolve tomato paste in chicken broth and add to crock-pot.

Add canned tomatoes and stir.

Add chicken, mix well, cover, and cook on low for 6–7 hours. Makes 6 servings.

This stew freezes beautifully.

Sweet and Spicy Drumsticks

2   tablespoons raw honey

2   teaspoons red chili flakes

2   tablespoons olive oil

½   teaspoon sea salt

½   teaspoon pepper

2   pounds chicken drumsticks

Preheat oven to 375 degrees F.

Toss honey, red chili flakes, olive oil, salt and pepper together in a Ziploc bag.

Add the chicken to the bag to coat chicken and refrigerate for at least 2 hours.

Lay drumsticks on a foil covered baking sheet. Place in the oven for 20 minutes, turning the drumsticks once during cooking time.

Broil for the last couple of minutes to add a bit of crispiness. Makes 4 servings.

These are excellent; great as a dinner, snack or appetizer!

POULTRY

Sweet Tamari Chicken

¼ cup fresh cilantro, leaves removed and finely chopped

1 large garlic clove, minced

1 teaspoon chili powder

⅓ cup tamari

3 tablespoons raw honey

¼ teaspoon sesame oil

⅓ cup olive oil

4 boneless, skinless chicken breasts

Mix cilantro, garlic, chili powder, tamari, honey, sesame oil and olive oil together in a large Ziploc bag. Add chicken to bag and marinate.

Refrigerate for at least 4 hours up to overnight.

When ready to cook, grill chicken over medium-high heat until a meat thermometer registers 160 degrees F when inserted into the thickest part. Makes 4 servings.

Lemon Chicken with Summer Squash

2   pounds boneless, skinless chicken breasts, cut into bite-sized pieces
1   sweet onion
1   large lemon
1   large summer squash
1   large zucchini
2   tablespoons coconut oil
1   tablespoon garlic powder
1   teaspoon pepper
1   teaspoon sea salt
4   cups chicken broth

A simple, easy, tasty meal.

Preheat oven to 350 degrees F.

Chop onion, squash and zucchini into bite-sized pieces. Slice a lemon into 6–8 crosswise slices.

Heat 2 tablespoons of coconut oil over medium heat in a Dutch oven. Sauté onion until soft.

Add chicken. Brown, stirring occasionally.

Add salt, garlic powder and pepper. Add squash, zucchini and lemon slices and mix well.

Add enough chicken broth to almost, but not quite, submerge ingredients.

Cover and place in the oven to bake for 60 minutes. Makes 4 servings.

Use lemon juice, lime juice, or vinegar to liven up a dish. It adds a nice fresh zing.

POULTRY

Spicy Turkey Meatloaf

1   pound ground turkey (dark meat)

1   pound ground turkey (breast meat)

2   chipotle chili peppers in adobe sauce, finely chopped,

plus 1 tablespoon of the adobe sauce

½   cup onion, finely chopped

½   cup fresh cilantro, leaves removed and finely chopped

½   cup almond flour

2   (8 ounce) cans tomato sauce

2   teaspoons dried parsley

1   teaspoon sea salt

½   teaspoon ground cumin

1   teaspoon dried oregano

1   teaspoon dried basil

½   teaspoon pepper

2   garlic cloves, minced

3   eggs, beaten

3   tablespoons Primal 51 Ketchup (recipe, page 72)

½   teaspoon hot sauce (optional)

Coconut oil to grease pan

Preheat oven to 350 degrees F.

Combine turkey, chilies, adobo sauce, onion, cilantro, flour, 1 can tomato sauce, parsley, salt, cumin, oregano, basil, pepper, garlic and eggs in a large bowl and mix to combine. Place turkey mixture in a 9×5-inch loaf pan greased with coconut oil. Bake uncovered for 40 minutes.

Combine 1 can tomato sauce, Primal 51 Ketchup, and hot sauce in a small bowl. Pour evenly over meat loaf. Bake uncovered an additional 30 minutes or until a meat thermometer registers 160 degrees F. Let stand 5 minutes at room temperature before slicing/serving. Makes 6 servings.

Almond-Crusted Chicken

1¼ cups sliced almonds

1 tablespoon dried thyme

2 teaspoons ground cumin

1 teaspoon pepper

¼ teaspoon sea salt

3 eggs, beaten

4 boneless, skinless chicken breasts

Olive oil

Preheat oven to 400 degrees F.

Place almonds in a large skillet over medium heat and cook for 2 minutes, stirring frequently. Transfer almonds to a plate and let cool.

Place almonds in a food processor with thyme, cumin, pepper and salt. Pulse to get coarse chop.

Set up a production line with beaten eggs in one bowl alongside crust mixture in a larger bowl.

Dip chicken breasts in egg mixture and drain excess egg back into the same bowl. Next, dredge chicken in the crust mixture and coat on both sides. Cover a baking sheet with foil then lightly grease the foil with olive oil. Place chicken on the baking sheet.

Drizzle chicken with olive oil and place in oven for about 20 minutes or until a meat thermometer registers 160 degrees F when inserted in the thickest part. Makes 4 servings.

This dish can also be a great appetizer; cut into bite-sized pieces and serve with toothpicks.

Turkey Chili

1 tablespoon coconut oil

1 large onion, chopped

½ cup of celery, chopped

½ cup red bell pepper, chopped

1 jalapeño, seeded and minced

3 garlic cloves, minced

3 cups cooked turkey or chicken, chopped into ½-inch pieces

4 cups chicken broth

2 (6-ounce) cans chopped green chilies

2 teaspoons ground cumin

2 tablespoons chili powder

½ teaspoon sea salt

½ teaspoon of pepper

1 cup of coconut milk

Cayenne pepper, to taste

½ cup fresh cilantro, leaves removed and finely chopped

Heat coconut oil in a large Dutch oven over medium-high heat. Add onion, celery, pepper, jalapeño and garlic and sauté for 15 minutes.

Add turkey or chicken, broth, green chilies, cumin, chili powder, salt, pepper, coconut milk and cayenne and bring to a boil. Lower heat and simmer. Cover and cook for 30 minutes.

Serve hot with cilantro sprinkled on top. Makes 6 servings.

A great way to use leftover cooked turkey or chicken! This chili freezes well.

Rosemary Chicken Thighs and Sweet Potatoes

8	chicken thighs, with skin
2	medium sweet potatoes, peeled, halved and sliced
½	cup coconut oil, melted
1	tablespoon dried rosemary
1	tablespoon garlic powder
1	tablespoon paprika
½	teaspoon pepper
½	teaspoon sea salt

Preheat oven to 375 degrees F.

Put chicken and potatoes in a large bowl. Add coconut oil to bowl and stir to coat all pieces of chicken and potatoes thoroughly.

Put chicken and potato pieces into a 13×9 glass baking dish.

Sprinkle with rosemary, garlic powder, paprika, pepper and salt.

Bake for about 30 minutes, uncovered. To ensure extra flavor and crispiness, baste chicken and potatoes every 10 minutes. Makes 4 servings.

This recipe is also great with bone-in chicken breasts with skin. The skin gets really crispy and tasty!

Fish and Seafood

These recipes are fairly simple and can be adjusted to use almost any type of fish you would like. Our family favorites are tilapia, salmon, swordfish, red snapper and tuna. Fish and seafood are very versatile; try any of the marinades or rubs on them to create great flavorful fillets.

Garlic Shrimp

2   pounds shrimp, peeled and deveined
(Costco sells bags of frozen, raw shrimp; the 21–24 count bags are great for this recipe. Thaw in a bowl of cool water for about 10 minutes before using.)
⅓   cup olive oil
4   garlic cloves, peeled
1   shallot, peeled and chopped
¼   teaspoon red pepper flakes
½   cup chicken broth
½   teaspoon sea salt
½   teaspoon pepper

Preheat oven to 375 degrees F.

Place shrimp in a 9×13 glass baking dish.

Place oil and garlic in a food processor or blender and pulse for 30–45 seconds, scraping down the sides as necessary. Add the shallot and red pepper flakes and pulse a few more times.

Coat the shrimp with the mixture, add broth, and mix well. Sprinkle with salt and pepper.

Bake for about 8 minutes until all shrimp are pink throughout. Do not overcook, these won't take very long.

Serve with sauce from the dish. Makes 6 servings.

Grilled Tuna with Olive Relish

Relish

½   cup parsley, chopped

⅓   cup pitted kalamata olives, chopped

¼   cup celery, finely chopped

1   garlic clove, minced

½   teaspoon dried oregano

2   tablespoons lemon juice

1   teaspoon olive oil

½   teaspoon sea salt

1   teaspoon pepper

Grilled Tuna

1   tablespoon olive oil

¼   teaspoon sea salt

¼   teaspoon pepper

1   pound tuna steak

Preheat grill to high heat.

Mix all relish ingredients in a medum bowl and set aside.

Rub oil, salt and pepper over both sides of tuna steaks and grill for 1 minute each side for rare tuna. Grill 2 minutes if you like your tuna cooked throughout a bit more.

Top with olive relish. Makes 4 servings.

I sometimes cheat and top with Trader Joe's Olive Tapenade instead of making it from scratch. Easy and delicious.

Ginger and Lime Tuna

2   (6-ounce) pieces sushi-grade tuna

1   handful fresh cilantro, stems removed and finely chopped

1   jalapeño, seeded and finely chopped

2   teaspoons fresh ginger, grated

1   garlic clove, minced

Juice of 2 limes

2   tablespoons tamari

Sea salt and pepper, to taste

¼   cup olive oil

1   ripe avocado, peeled, pitted and sliced

Combine the cilantro, jalapeño, ginger, garlic, lime juice, tamari, salt, pepper and 2 tablespoons of the olive oil in a medium bowl and whisk to combine. Set aside.

Place a large skillet over high heat and coat with the remaining 2 tablespoons of olive oil. Season the tuna generously with salt and pepper. Lay the tuna in the hot oil and sear for 1 minute on each side to form a slight crust. Cook an extra minute if you like your tuna cooked more. (We like ours rare.)

Pour ½ of the cilantro mixture into the pan to coat the fish. Remove from heat.

Slice tuna and place on a serving plate along with the avocado slices. Drizzle with remaining cilantro sauce and serve immediately. Makes 4 servings.

FRAMPTON FAMILY FAVORITE!

This is amazing; a great dish to serve at dinner parties!

Basil Salmon Fillets

4   salmon fillets with skin

6   basil leaves, chopped

1   tablespoon capers, drained

1   shallot, chopped

2   tablespoons olive oil

1   tablespoon white wine vinegar

Pepper, to taste

In a large non-stick skillet, heat 1 tablespoon of olive oil over medium heat. Add salmon and cook uncovered, flesh-side-down first, for about 3 minutes. Flip and cook for 3 more minutes or to desired doneness.

While salmon is cooking, combine basil, capers, shallot, 1 tablespoon olive oil, vinegar and pepper in a small bowl and mix well. Pour the mixture over the salmon just as it comes off the heat. Makes 4 servings.

This is terrific with roasted asparagus.

Pistachio-Crusted Swordfish

4	swordfish steaks (about 6 oz. each)
1	cup vegetable broth
1	cup pistachios, dry-roasted, shelled
⅓	cup fresh cilantro
2	tablespoons olive oil
¼	teaspoon pepper
¼	teaspoon sea salt

Preheat oven to 400 degrees F.

Pulse the pistachios in a food processor for 20 seconds to a coarse consistency.

Finely chop the cilantro and place in a medium mixing bowl along with the pistachios, olive oil, salt and pepper. Mix well and set aside.

Place the swordfish fillets in one layer in a large, foil-lined baking dish. Season both sides with salt and pepper.

Place about 1 tablespoon of the pistachio mixture on the top of each fillet, spreading it evenly on each piece of fish. Press the mixture slightly into the fish. Add broth to the baking pan (do not pour the broth on top of the fish) and bake for 8 minutes.

Preheat the broiler and place the broiling rack in the top third or the center of the oven. When broiler is hot, broil the fish 1–2 minutes or until topping is golden brown but not dry. Makes 4 servings.

Adding broth to the baking dish helps to create steam in the oven and keeps the fish moist. Whenever you broil fish, keep an eye on it to prevent overcooking.

Salmon Fillets with Basil and Ginger

2   pounds salmon fillets with skin

1   cup orange juice

¼   cup tamari

2   tablespoons fresh ginger, minced

2   tablespoons fresh basil, finely chopped

2-3 oranges

1   cup red bell pepper strips

1   bulb fennel, stems and fronds removed, sliced

1   teaspoon dark sesame oil

Sea salt and pepper, to taste

Mix orange juice, tamari, ginger and basil in mixing bowl. Add salmon to bowl and cover. Marinate salmon for 1–2 hours in the refrigerator. Remove 30 minutes before cooking to let fish return to room temperature.

Meanwhile, use a sharp knife to prepare the oranges. Place the oranges on a cutting board and slice off the top and bottom so that the orange sits flat. Slice off the sides of the orange peel. Hold the peeled oranges over a small bowl and cut between the membranes to release the orange segments into a bowl.

Combine oranges, bell pepper, fennel, sesame oil and salt in a medium bowl. This can be prepared at least 1 hour ahead of time.

Preheat oven to 400 degrees F.

Lay marinated salmon in a large baking dish in a single layer, skin-side-down and cook for about 15 minutes or until opaque in color and firm to the touch. You may also broil it on a greased broiling pan for about 12–14 minutes. Cook to desired degree of doneness.

Serve with the orange-bell pepper mixture. Makes 4 servings.

Pan-Seared Salmon
with Avocado Sauce

2   large avocados, peeled, pitted and roughly chopped

3   tablespoons lime juice

3-4 tablespoons olive oil, plus additional oil

1   tablespoon shallots, minced

1   tablespoon fresh parsley, minced

2   teaspoons Dijon mustard

2   pounds of salmon fillets with skin

Sea salt and pepper, to taste

Put avocado pieces and lime juice into a food processor and pulse until blended.

Slowly add olive oil down the feed tube, pulsing several times, until you reach desired consistency.

Add minced shallots, parsley, mustard, salt and pepper and pulse to blend. Set aside.

Coat the bottom of a large skillet with some oil and heat on medium-high. Season the salmon with salt and pepper. Carefully lay the salmon into the pan, skin-side-up. Cook the salmon for about 3–4 minutes per side for medium doneness.

Serve salmon with avocado sauce. Makes 4 servings.

Build your diet around the Paleo basics every day: meat, healthy fats and vegetables.

Crock-Pot Jambalaya

4   tablespoons coconut oil, plus more as needed

1   onion, chopped

1   red bell pepper, chopped

3   garlic cloves, minced

4   boneless, skinless chicken breasts, cut into 2-inch pieces

1   pound Linguica sausage, cut into 1-inch pieces

1   (16 ounce) can diced tomatoes with their juices

4   cups chicken broth

2   tablespoons Cajun Seasoning (recipe, page 71)

1   cup baby spinach

1   pound raw medium or jumbo shrimp, peeled

2   cups Cauliflower "Rice" (see note with recipe, page 113)

Heat 2 tablespoons of the coconut oil in a large skillet over medium heat. Add onions, bell pepper and garlic and sauté 10–15 minutes or until onions and pepper are softened. Add to crock-pot.

Add 1–2 teaspoons coconut oil to the skillet over medium heat. Add the chicken and cook 5–8 minutes until browned, turning occasionally. Add chicken to crock-pot.

Add Linguica pieces to the crock-pot.

Add tomatoes and their juices, chicken broth and Cajun Seasoning to crock-pot. Cook on low for about 3½ hours.

Add 1–2 teaspoons coconut oil to the skillet and sauté shrimp about 5 minutes. Add shrimp, spinach and Cauliflower "Rice" to crock-pot and cook 30 minutes longer. Makes 6 servings.

Freezes well.

Fish "Tacos" with Slaw

4   cups green cabbage, thinly sliced

1   cup carrots, grated

1   tomato, chopped

½   cup scallions, chopped

2   tablespoons lime juice

2   tablespoons olive oil

1   teaspoon sea salt

4   tilapia fillets, about 6 ounces each

1   tablespoon chili powder

Lettuce "boats" (romaine lettuce hearts)

Combine cabbage, carrots, tomato and scallions in a large bowl. Add lime juice, 1 tablespoon oil and ½ teaspoon salt.

Heat remaining olive oil in a large nonstick skillet over medium-high heat. Sprinkle fish evenly with chili powder and remaining ½ teaspoon of salt. Add fish to skillet and cook uncovered 3 minutes on each side, until fish flakes easily with a fork.

Remove fish from the skillet, cool slightly then break up the fish into bite-sized pieces.

To make "tacos," fill each lettuce leaf with about ¼ cup slaw and about half of a tilapia fillet. Makes 4 servings.

Spicy Tilapia Fillets

4-6 tilapia fillets, about 6 ounces each

2   tablespoons olive oil

2   teaspoons chipotle pepper seasoning

1   teaspoon pepper

Pinch sea salt

2   tablespoons lime juice

½   red onion, finely chopped

6   garlic cloves, minced

1   large jalapeño, seeded and finely chopped

2   tablespoons tequila

2   tomatoes, diced

1   avocado, peeled, pitted and diced

1   bunch fresh cilantro, leaves removed and finely chopped

Preheat oven to 350 degrees F.

Season fish fillets with chipotle, pepper and salt.

Heat olive oil in a large skillet. Add tilapia and cook uncovered over medium heat, about 2–3 minutes or until light golden brown. Place fish in one layer in a large baking dish, cover with foil to keep warm and set aside.

Deglaze the skillet with lime juice (scraping loose all the bits).

Add onion, garlic and jalapeño pepper to skillet. Sauté about 10 minutes or until onion is soft and liquid from the onion has evaporated.

Add the tequila. Mix well and cook for about 5 minutes. (Note: this will burn off the alcohol; what's left is just the flavor of the tequila.)

Pour mixture over fillets in the baking dish and bake uncovered for about 8 minutes or until cooked through.

Combine tomatoes, avocado and cilantro in a medium bowl and serve alongside the fish. Makes 4 servings.

Sea Scallops with Spaghetti Squash

1   medium spaghetti squash, sliced in half and seeded
2   tablespoons coconut oil
20   (approximately) shucked sea scallops
½   teaspoon sea salt
½   teaspoon pepper
¼   cup dry red wine
1   sweet onion, chopped
3   garlic cloves, minced
3   fresh tomatoes, chopped
2   teaspoons Italian seasoning
½   cup fresh basil, chopped

Heat oven to 350 degrees F.

Place spaghetti squash halves in a 13×9 glass baking dish, skin-side-up, with enough water to cover the bottom of the dish by about ½-inch. Bake uncovered for 45 minutes.

While squash is cooking, heat coconut oil in a large skillet over medium-high heat. Sprinkle scallops with salt and pepper, and sear about 3 minutes per side or until golden brown. Do not overcook. Remove from skillet and set aside.

Deglaze skillet with red wine for about 2–4 minutes. Add onion and garlic and sauté 5–10 minutes stirring frequently until tender.

Add chopped tomatoes and Italian seasoning to the skillet and cook 1–2 minutes or until flavors are blended and the mixture is warm. Add scallops and basil and simmer over low heat 5–10 minutes or until scallops are opaque (cooked through) but not dry. Remove from heat, cover with foil to keep warm and set aside.

Remove the squash from the oven and let cool 5 minutes or until easy to handle. Use a fork to scrape out the squash and place an equal portion on each serving plate.

Spoon scallop tomato mixture over spaghetti squash. Makes 4 servings.

Lime Tilapia

Coconut oil, as needed

4   tilapia fillets or any other white fish fillets, about 6 ounces each

Juice of 1 lime

1   tablespoon ghee (recipe, page 63), melted

2   garlic cloves, minced

1   tablespoon fresh parsley, finely chopped or 1 teaspoon dried parsley

Sea salt and pepper, to taste

Preheat oven to 375 degrees F.

Coat a 13×9 baking dish with coconut oil. Place fillets in baking dish.

Pour lime juice over fillets and then drizzle ghee on top.

Top with garlic, parsley, salt and pepper.

Bake uncovered 12–15 minutes or until fish is opaque and flakes easily with a fork. Timing will depend on thickness of the fillets. Makes 4 servings.

FRAMPTON FAMILY FAVORITE!

Great with Spicy Salsa (see recipe, page 51).

FISH AND SEAFOOD

Spicy Lime Salmon

Coconut oil, to grease baking dish

4   salmon fillets, about 6 ounces each

2   tablespoons olive oil

3   limes; 2 cut in half, 1 cut crosswise into thin slices

1   teaspoon sea salt

1   teaspoon chipotle pepper seasoning

Preheat oven to 500 degrees F.

Rinse salmon and pat dry. Grease a large baking dish with coconut oil. Place salmon in the baking dish in one layer and rub each fillet generously with the 2 tablespoons of olive oil. Squeeze the juice of 2 limes over the fillets.

Sprinkle the fillets with the salt and chipotle pepper and then place about 3 or 4 slices of lime on top of each fillet.

Turn oven down to 300 degrees F and bake about 10 minutes or until opaque and cooked through, but not dry. Makes 4 servings.

I rarely enjoy leftover fish, but this is an exception. The leftover salmon is great over a salad the next day.

Spicy Tilapia with Pineapple Relish

1 tablespoon of Emeril's Essence Seasoning or make your own Cajun Seasoning (recipe, page 71)

¼ teaspoon sea salt

¼ teaspoon pepper

4-6 tilapia fillets, about 6 ounces each

2 tablespoons olive oil

Pineapple Relish

1½ cups fresh pineapple, chopped

⅓ cup red onion, finely diced

1 tomato, diced

1-2 tablespoons unfiltered apple cider

2 tablespoons fresh cilantro, leaves removed and finely chopped

1 jalapeño pepper, seeded and finely chopped

Juice of 1 lime

Combine Cajun Seasoning, salt and pepper in a small bowl or plate. Coat the fish evenly with spice mixture.

Heat oil in a large nonstick skillet over medium-high heat. Add fish to pan, and cook for about 2 minutes on each side or to desired degree of doneness. Remove from heat and cover with foil to keep warm.

Combine pineapple, onion, tomato, apple cider, cilantro, jalapeño and lime juice in a large bowl and whisk to blend. Serve alongside the fish. Makes 4 servings.

The Pineapple Relish really makes the dish. We enjoy it with many other fish and chicken recipes!

FISH AND SEAFOOD

Pork

Grill it, broil it, braise it, roast or smoke it. Pork is so versatile and easy to cook. Some cuts cook quickly and others can cook slowly—relatively unattended—in a smoker or crock-pot. The recipes here are a springboard for your own favorite seasonings; don't be shy! Get out the spices and herbs.

Lemon and Thyme Pork Chops

4   boneless pork chops, about 1 inch thick

1   tablespoon coconut oil, melted

Juice of 1 lemon

2   teaspoons dried thyme

Sea salt and pepper, to taste

Coat both sides of pork chops with coconut oil. Cook the pork in one layer in a large skillet over high heat uncovered. Cook about 2 minutes on each side. Remove pork chops from pan and set aside.

Cut the lemon in half and squeeze juices into the pan, discarding lemon seeds. Add thyme, salt and pepper to taste. Add pork chops back to the pan and cook covered for about 10 minutes or until a meat thermometer inserted in the thickest part registers 145 degrees F.

Remove from heat and let rest 2 minutes before serving. Makes 4 servings.

Slow-Cooked Pork Shoulder with Apricots

1   4-5 pound pork shoulder or butt, trimmed of visible fat
2   tablespoons olive oil
1   apple, peeled and diced
1½ cups dried apricots, chopped
1   onion, chopped
2   celery stalks, chopped
¼   cup raisins
½   cup chicken broth
½   cup dry white wine

Coating for pork
¼   cup almond flour
2   teaspoons garlic power
2   teaspoons pepper
1   tablespoon dried parsley flakes

Combine flour, garlic powder, pepper and parsley. Coat the pork shoulder or butt with the almond flour mixture. Brown it in a large, deep skillet with about 2 tablespoon olive oil, uncovered for about 10–15 minutes, turning frequently, until deep golden brown on all sides.

After browning the pork, put it into a large crock-pot. Cover the pork with apple, apricots, onion, celery, raisins, chicken broth and wine. Cook on low for 6–8 hours or until pork is tender.

Transfer pork to a grooved cutting board, cover loosely with foil and let stand for 5 minutes or until cool enough to handle. Pull pork apart using a fork and serve it with crock-pot juices. Makes 8–10 servings.

Sweet and yummy.

Poblano Pork Stew

3 poblano peppers

4 tablespoons olive oil

½ tablespoon dried thyme

1 onion, diced

1 red bell pepper, halved, seeded and diced

3 garlic cloves, minced

2-3 pounds pork tenderloin, trimmed and cut into 1-inch cubes

1 tablespoon paprika

4 cups chicken broth

½ teaspoon dried chili flakes

2 teaspoons lime juice

½ tablespoon dried marjoram

1 cup dry white wine

Sea salt and pepper, to taste

Preheat oven to 350 degrees F.

To roast poblano peppers:
Place peppers on a foil-lined baking sheet and coat peppers liberally with olive oil. Roast until skin is lightly charred on all sides, turning the peppers once or twice. Place peppers in a brown paper bag and fold the bag to seal. Let the peppers cool for at least 20 minutes. This will allow the peppers to steam so that the skin comes off easily.

To remove skins:
Remove skins from poblano peppers with your fingers, using a gentle tug as needed. Do not (as many recipes advise) run the peppers under running water to help remove skins; this also removes the delicious charred flavor from the peppers. Remove stems, halve the peppers lengthwise and discard seeds and dice.

Preheat Dutch oven over medium heat. Add 2 tablespoons olive oil. Add thyme, onion, red pepper, poblano peppers and garlic and cook uncovered, stirring frequently, for about 10 minutes or until onions and bell pepper have softened.

Poblano peppers are mild in flavor and are great in sauces, stews and salsas.

While vegetables are cooking, add all the diced pork into a large bowl and sprinkle with paprika and toss to coat pork well. Set aside.

Transfer all of the Dutch oven contents to a plate or bowl and set aside. Add 1 tablespoon of olive oil to the Dutch oven and add half the pork pieces to the pot. Sear for 3–4 minutes, stirring occasionally, until the pork is brown on all sides.

When the first batch has browned, transfer to a plate or bowl. Add the second half of the pork and repeat, adding more oil if needed.

Transfer all the pork pieces and vegetables from the plates back into the Dutch oven and add chicken broth, chili flakes, lime juice, marjoram and wine. Combine the ingredients and bring to a boil.

Move Dutch oven to a preheated 350 degree F oven and cook for 1–2 hours, stirring once or twice during cooking time. Add salt and pepper to taste. Makes 6 servings.

PORK

Pork Chops with Golden Raisin Sauce

2 tablespoons olive oil

4 pork chops, about ½ inch thick

Sea salt and pepper, to taste

½ cup onion, finely chopped

4 garlic cloves, minced

1 cup chicken broth

½ cup dry white wine

2 tablespoons Dijon mustard

1 teaspoon drained prepared horseradish

1 tablespoon raw honey

2 tablespoons fresh parsley, chopped, or 1 tablespoon dried parsley

1 cup golden raisins

Heat olive oil over medium heat in a large skillet. Add pork chops to skillet, sprinkle with salt and pepper and cook on each side for about 2 minutes. Remove from skillet and set aside.

Add onion and garlic to the same skillet and cook, stirring frequently, 2–3 minutes or until slightly softened. Add broth, wine, mustard, horseradish, honey, parsley and golden raisins. Cook, uncovered, for about 5 minutes or until the liquid in the pan has reduced by about half.

Return pork chops to the skillet and simmer, covered, over low heat for 10–15 minutes or until cooked through but not dry. Makes 4 servings.

FRAMPTON FAMILY FAVORITE!

This raisin sauce is awesome!

Chorizo-Stuffed Pork Loin

1   5-6 pound pork loin roast
1   pound chorizo, chopped into ¼–½ inch pieces
1   teaspoon dried rosemary
1   tablespoon dried parsley
1   teaspoon dried sage
1   teaspoon dried thyme
2   garlic cloves, minced
1   teaspoon sea salt
½   cup ghee (recipe, page 63), melted

Knowing how to butterfly a roast opens up all kinds of options: Watch the butcher, watch a video, practice and you can start trying different stuffing combinations.

Preheat oven to 450 degrees F.

To prepare a roll-cut butterflied roast, check the National Pork Board's website which includes an excellent video, "Butterflying a Pork Loin Roast" (http://www.youtube.com/watch?v=Fz391Urnk30).

Place chorizo on the inside of the pork, leaving a 1-inch border on all sides so the chorizo doesn't fall out. Top chorizo with rosemary, parsley, sage, thyme and garlic. Roll the pork loin into a cylindar shape and use butcher's twine around the stuffed pork to hold the stuffing in place.

Coat the outside of the roast with ghee and sprinkle with salt to taste. Place the roast on a roasting rack in a large, shallow roasting pan. Roast for 10 minutes then lower oven temperature to 350 degrees F and continue to cook 50–60 minutes or until a meat thermometer inserted in the thickest part registers 145 degrees F.

Remove from oven and transfer the roast to a grooved cutting board. Cover loosely with foil and let rest for 10 minutes before slicing and serving. Makes 8–10 servings.

Stuffed pork roast is a festive choice for holidays and dinner parties.

Apple-Shallot Pork Chops

4   pork chops, about 1-inch thick
2   apples
5   tablespoons coconut oil
2   shallots, sliced thin
¼   cup dry white wine
Cinnamon and sea salt, to taste
Toasted slivered almonds

Peel, halve, core the apple then cut into thin crosswise slices.

Heat 4 tablespoons of the coconut oil in a large skillet over medium heat and add the apples and shallots. Cook uncovered, stirring occasionally, 5–8 minutes or until the apples are tender. Transfer the apples and shallots to a bowl and set aside.

Add the remaining tablespoon of coconut oil to the skillet over medium-high heat. Sprinkle cinnamon and salt on both sides of the pork chops and place them in the hot skillet. Sear on each side for 2 minutes.

Add wine to pan. Bring wine to a boil to cook off the alcohol. After adding the wine, add the apple-shallot mixture and pork chops back to the pan. Cover and cook over low heat for 10–12 minutes, depending on the thickness of the pork chops. The internal temperature of the thickest chop should be at least 145 degrees F. Remove pork chops from the pan.

Serve the pork chops with plenty of the apple-shallot mixture and add a sprinkle of slivered toasted almonds on top. Makes 4 servings.

My kids love the sweet sauce more than the actual pork chops!

Pork Stew with Salsa Verde

2   tablespoons coconut oil

1   4 pound pork roast, cut into 2-inch pieces

3   sweet onions, chopped

4   garlic cloves, minced

1   cup carrots, grated

1   tablespoon paprika

1   teaspoon ground cumin

2   tablespoons chili powder

1   red bell pepper, chopped

1   jalapeño pepper, seeded and finely diced

1   (12 ounce) jar Salsa Verde (we like Trader Joe's salsa verde)

Juice from one lime

2   cups chicken broth

1   cup fresh cilantro, leaves removed and finely chopped

FRAMPTON FAMILY FAVORITE!

Freezes well.

Preheat oven 350 degrees F.

Place coconut oil in Dutch oven and place over medium-high heat. Working in batches, add pork and cook each batch, stirring frequently, about 5 minutes or until browned. As each batch browns, transfer it to a plate and set aside.

Add onions to pan and cook about 10–15 minutes or until softened and light golden brown, stirring frequently. Add garlic and cook another 2 minutes.

Add grated carrots, paprika, cumin, chili powder, red pepper and jalapeño pepper. Cook, stirring frequently, for about 10–15 minutes. Mixture may seem thick but keep stirring. Add 1 jar Salsa Verde, lime juice, chicken broth and cilantro. Bring to boil and return pork to pot. Place in oven and cook, covered for 2–3 hours, stirring once or twice. Makes 6 servings.

Serve as is or over some Mashed Sweet Potatoes (see recipe, page 103). This stuff is so good!

Slow-Roasted Pork Shoulder

1   tablespoon dried oregano
2   tablespoons garlic powder
2   tablespoons chili powder
2   teaspoons ground cumin
1   teaspoon cayenne pepper
1   tablespoon paprika
1   teaspoon sea salt
2   red bell peppers, diced
2   large onions, diced
1   tablespoon coconut oil
1   (28 ounce) can diced tomatoes with their juices
1   4-pound bone-in pork shoulder
2   tablespoons raw honey

Mix oregano, garlic powder, chili powder, cumin, cayenne pepper, paprika and salt in a small bowl and generously rub on all sides of the pork shoulder.

Cook the peppers and onions uncovered in a large skillet over medium heat with the coconut oil, stirring frequently, for 5 minutes or until softened. Transfer them to the bottom of a crock-pot. Add the tomatoes and mix.

Add the pork shoulder, fat-side-down on top of the mixture.

Cook on low for 6–7 hours or until pork is tender and falling off the bone. Drizzle honey over the pork and serve. Makes 6–8 servings.

Change this recipe up by adding any herbs, spices or sauces that you like. Pork shoulder is so versatile!

Lemon Dijon Pork Tenderloin

2   pork tenderloins (about 1 pound each)

Grated zest of 1 lemon

¾   cup lemon juice

½   cup olive oil plus 2 tablespoons

3   garlic cloves, minced

2   teaspoons dried rosemary

2   teaspoons dried thyme

2   tablespoons Dijon mustard

2   teaspoons sea salt

Sea salt and pepper, to taste

Combine the lemon zest, lemon juice, olive oil, garlic, rosemary, thyme, mustard and a dash of salt in a large Ziploc bag.

Add the pork tenderloins and turn to coat with the marinade. Marinate pork in the refrigerator for at least 3 hours, but preferably overnight.

Preheat oven to 400 degrees F.

Remove the tenderloins from the marinade and discard the marinade.

Sprinkle the tenderloins generously with salt and pepper.

Heat 2 tablespoons of the olive oil in a large oven-proof skillet over medium-high heat. Sear the pork tenderloins on all sides until golden brown, about 2 minutes per side.

Place the skillet in the oven and roast the tenderloins for about 10–15 minutes or until a meat thermometer inserted into the thickest part registers 145 degrees. Do not overcook.

Transfer to a platter, cover loosely with foil and let meat rest for 10 minutes before slicing. Makes 6 servings.

FRAMPTON FAMILY FAVORITE!

PORK

Baked Pork Chops with Mustard, Rosemary and Garlic

Marinade

1 tablespoon dried rosemary

2 tablespoons Dijon mustard

Juice and grated zest of 1 lemon

2 garlic cloves, minced

¼ teaspoon sea salt

¼ teaspoon pepper

¼ cup olive oil

4 pork chops, bone-in

¼ cup chicken broth

2 tablespoons olive oil to coat skillet

Mix all marinade ingredients together in a large bowl and toss pork chops to coat. Cover and refrigerate for at least 2 hours or overnight.

Remove from refrigerator 30 minutes before cooking to let return to room temperature.

Preheat oven to 450 degrees F.

Drizzle olive oil in a large skillet over medium-high heat and sear chops for 2–3 minutes each side until golden brown. Transfer chops to a foil-lined 9×13 baking dish and place chops in one layer.

Pour the broth into the baking dish and swish the dish if necessary so that the broth surrounds the chops.

Bake, uncovered, in the oven for about 7 minutes or until a meat thermometer inserted into the thickest part registers 145 degrees F. Remove from the oven, cover loosely with foil and let stand for 5 minutes. Makes 4 servings.

Roast Pork Tenderloin with Lime and Chili

1-2 pounds pork tenderloin
3 tablespoons raw honey
2 tablespoons chili powder
Juice and grated zest of 1 lime
1 teaspoon garlic powder

Mix honey, chili powder, lime juice, lime zest and garlic powder into a large Ziploc bag. Add the pork, seal the bag, and marinate at least 2 hours or overnight.

Preheat oven to 425 degrees F or preheat grill to medium-high.

Remove the pork from the Ziploc bag and discard the marinade. If roasting the pork, place it on a rack in a roasting pan and cook for 5 minutes. Lower heat to 350 degrees F and continue to cook for 15 minutes or until a meat thermometer inserted in the thickest part registers 150 degrees F. If grilling, cook about 15 minutes, flipping every 5 minutes.

Transfer pork to a grooved cutting board, cover loosely with foil and let it rest 5 minutes before slicing. Makes 4 servings.

FRAMPTON FAMILY FAVORITE!

Pork tenderloin cooks quickly, marries well with a variety of spices and herbs, and as its name implies, it is very tender.

PORK

Pork Pot Roast with Tomatoes and Leeks

4 tablespoons coconut oil

Sea salt and pepper, to taste

1 4-5 pound pork roast

¼ cup coconut flour

6 carrots, peeled and chopped

5 celery stalks, finely chopped

2 leeks, rinsed and chopped

2 onions, chopped

1-2 cups dry red wine

1½ cups chicken broth, or more if needed

1 (28 ounce) can diced tomatoes with their juices

1 tablespoon dried thyme

6 garlic cloves, minced

In a large Dutch oven, add coconut oil and heat over medium heat.

Sprinkle salt and pepper all over the roast. Roll the seasoned roast in coconut flour on a baking sheet or platter. Sear the roast in the Dutch oven uncovered for about 20 minutes, turning frequently, until the roast is golden brown. Remove the roast from the Dutch oven and add the carrots, celery, leeks and onions. Cook over medium heat uncovered, stirring frequently about 15–20 minutes or until softened and golden brown.

Preheat oven to 350 degrees F. (Delete this step if using a crock-pot.) Add the wine, chicken broth, tomatoes, thyme, garlic and a bit more salt and pepper. Stir well and bring to a boil.

Place roast back into Dutch oven or into a crock-pot. Pour the vegetable mixture over the pork. If you keep the roast in a Dutch oven, place in the preheated 350 degree oven for 2½ to 3 hours, covered, until pork is fork-tender. Stir the mixture several times as the roast cooks. If the vegetable mixture seems too thick, add extra chicken broth to reach desired consistency. If using a crock-pot, cook on low for 6–7 hours or until pork is fork-tender. Makes 8–10 servings.

Honey-Grilled Pork Loin

⅔ cup tamari
1 teaspoon ground ginger
1 garlic clove, minced
1 teaspoon coriander
2 pounds boneless pork tenderloin
½ cup raw honey
1½ tablespoons sesame oil

Combine tamari, ginger, garlic and coriander and pour into large Ziploc bag. Place pork tenderloins in bag. Refrigerate 3 hours or more.

Remove pork from Ziploc bag; discard marinade.

Preheat the grill to medium.

Combine honey and sesame oil in a small saucepan. Cook over low heat until honey dissolves.

Grill tenderloins, basting with honey mixture frequently. Grill about 20–25 minutes or until a meat thermometer inserted in the thickest part registers 145 degrees F.

Remove from grill, cover loosely with foil to keep warm, and let rest for 5 minutes before slicing. Makes 4 servings.

BBQ Pulled Pork

1   tablespoon olive oil

2   medium onions, diced

2   tablespoons chili powder

1   tablespoon ground cumin

1   tablespoon paprika

½   teaspoon cayenne

½   cup chicken broth

1   cup Primal 51 Ketchup (recipe, page 72)

¾   cup cider vinegar

¼   cup Dijon or yellow mustard

2   tablespoons tomato paste

1   chipotle pepper in adobo sauce, minced, plus 1 tablespoon adobo sauce

1   5-6 pound pork shoulder or butt, trimmed of visible fat

Preheat oven to 300 degrees F.

Heat oil in a large Dutch oven over medium-low heat. Add onions and cook, stirring occasionally, until lightly browned and very soft, about 20 minutes.

Increase heat to medium-high. Add chili powder, cumin, paprika, and cayenne. Cook, stirring frequently, until fragrant, about 2 minutes.

Add broth, Primal 51 Ketchup, vinegar, mustard, tomato paste, chipotle pepper and adobo sauce. Bring to a boil.

Reduce heat to medium-low and simmer, uncovered, stirring occasionally, until the sauce is slightly thickened, 10–15 minutes.

Meanwhile, trim all visible fat from the pork. Add the pork to the Dutch oven and spoon sauce over it.

Cover the Dutch oven and place in oven. Bake for 2 hours. Turn the pork over, cover, and bake for 2 more hours.

BBQ sauces are usually high in sugar. This one has some sweetness, but is definitely a Paleo-friendly version. If you want it sweeter, add some honey to the recipe.

Pork should be fork-tender and falling apart. If not, return to oven for an additional 30–60 minutes.

Transfer the pork to a large, deep bowl or platter.

Heat the sauce in the Dutch oven over medium-high heat and simmer uncovered about 10 minutes or until mixture has reduced slightly.

Pull the pork apart into long shreds using two forks.

Add the sauce to the meat. Stir to combine.

This dish can also be made in a crock-pot:
Mix all the ingredients (except the pork) together. Place the pork in the crock-pot and cover with mixture. Cook on low for 7–8 hours. You can do all the prep the night before and place the crock-pot insert into the refrigerator. Then the next morning, turn on the crock-pot and dinner will be ready when you get home from work. Makes 8–10 servings.

Beef

Beef's versatility makes it a delicious choice for all occasions. From an elegant dinner with filet roast to a quick weeknight meal of Sloppy Joes.

If you are able, always try to purchase grass fed beef. Grass fed beef is more flavorful and is Paleo recommended. Purchasing grass fed beef often provides an opportunity to support local farmers whose methods of raising and processing beef are often considered more humane and environmentally sustainable.

Sloppy Joes

1   onion, chopped
1   red pepper, chopped
2   tablespoons olive oil
4   garlic cloves, minced
2   pounds ground beef
1   (28 ounce) can tomato puree
2   tablespoons chili powder
2   tablespoons tomato paste
2   tablespoons Primal 51 Ketchup (recipe, page 72)
1   teaspoon ground mustard
1   teaspoon pepper
2   teaspoons red wine vinegar

Freezes well.

Sauté onions and peppers in olive oil in a large skillet over medium heat for about 10 minutes. Add garlic and cook another 5 minutes.

Add ground beef and cook through.

Add tomato puree, chili powder, tomato paste, ketchup, mustard, pepper and vinegar to beef mixture. Mix well and simmer on low about 30 minutes. Makes 6 servings.

FRAMPTON FAMILY FAVORITE!

Serve Sloppy Joes in a bowl on its own or over a bed or fresh arugula or other salad greens and chopped tomatoes.

Grilled Flank Steak with Pineapple Salsa

1-2 pounds flank steak
1 tablespoon olive oil
1 teaspoon chipotle chili seasoning
4 slices of pineapple
1 cup red bell peppers, chopped
½ cup red onion, chopped
¼ cup fresh cilantro, chopped
Juice of one lime
1 avocado, peeled, pitted and chopped

Preheat the grill.

Mix oil and chipotle powder in a small dish and coat steak well.

Grill for about 10–12 minutes, flipping once. Transfer to a plate, cover with foil to keep warm and let rest for 10 minutes. Grill the pineapple slices for 2–3 minutes per side.

Cut the pineapple into small chunks and add bell peppers, red onion, cilantro, lime juice and avocado. Mix well.

Slice the steak thinly, making sure to cut a flank steak against the grain. Serve with the pineapple salsa. Makes 4 servings.

Grilled Skirt Steak and Sweet Balsamic Onions

1½ pounds skirt steak

3 tablespoons tamari

2 teaspoons raw honey

¼ teaspoon cayenne pepper

2 garlic cloves, minced

1 teaspoon fresh ginger, grated

1 teaspoon sea salt

2-3 tablespoons balsamic vinegar

2 large sweet onions

In a Ziploc bag, add all ingredients, except the balsamic vinegar and onions. Massage the beef with the marinade. Let marinate for at least 1 hour or up to overnight.

Preheat the grill to high.

Remove the steak from the marinade, place on the grill and cook about 3 minutes per side. Transfer steak from the grill to a platter, cover with foil to keep warm and let it rest for 5 minutes.

While the steak is resting, slice the onions into thick slices and coat sides liberally with balsamic vinegar. Grill over medium high heat, about 2–4 minutes per side. Slice the steak and serve with the onions. Makes 4 servings.

Grilled onions are sweet and tender; we make them all summer long!

Sunday Roast

6	garlic cloves
1	sweet onion, coarsely chopped
¼	cup olive oil
1	teaspoon sea salt
2	teaspoons pepper
1	4-5 pound rib eye roast

Preheat oven to 400 degrees F.

In a food processor, combine all ingredients (except beef) and pulse to a creamy paste. Adjust olive oil if needed.

Rub the paste all over the roast, working it on top, bottom, and sides. Place any remaining paste on top as a "crust." Add extra pepper on top if desired.

Let the roast sit for 10 minutes with rub before placing on a roasting rack and putting into oven.

Roast for 15 minutes.

Reduce heat to 350 degrees F and cook another hour.

Insert a thermometer in the center. For medium-rare, remove from oven when temperature reads 135–140 degrees F.

Allow to rest at room temperature covered loosely with foil for 10 minutes before slicing. Makes 8 servings.

FRAMPTON FAMILY FAVORITE!

This is the Frampton family holiday roast; delicious!

BEEF

183

Stuffed Peppers

2   tablespoons olive oil and more to coat peppers

1   eggplant, peeled and chopped into ½-inch cubes

1   sweet onion, finely chopped

1   red pepper, finely chopped

1   medium zucchini, finely chopped

1   cup mushrooms, finely chopped

3   garlic cloves, minced

1   pound ground beef (or ground turkey)

2   tablespoons tomato paste

¼   cup chicken broth

1   tablespoon dried basil

1   teaspoon sea salt

1   teaspoon pepper

6   cubanelle peppers, stem ends removed and seeds discarded

Preheat oven to 375 degrees F.

Heat oil in a large skillet over medium heat. Add eggplant, onion, red pepper, zucchini, mushrooms and garlic and cook, stirring frequently, about 15–20 minutes or until most of the juices from the vegetables have evaporated and the vegetables are beginning to turn golden brown.

Add ground beef and cook through.

Add tomato paste, broth, basil, salt and pepper. Combine thoroughly and remove from heat. Cool for about 5–10 minutes.

Stuff each cubanelle pepper with meat mixture and then coat with olive oil all over the outside of the pepper.

Place in a 9×13 baking dish and bake for 30 minutes. Makes 6 servings.

I love using cubanelle peppers because they are thin and soften quickly; feel free to use red bell or green peppers instead.

Savory Bolognese Sauce

2 tablespoons coconut oil

2 sweet onions, finely chopped

1 cup carrots, grated

4 celery stalks, finely chopped

1 small zucchini, shredded

4 garlic cloves, minced

2 pounds ground beef

1 teaspoon sea salt

1 teaspoon pepper

1 (6 ounce) can tomato paste

2 cups dry red wine

4-6 cups water

2 bay leaves

1 teaspoon dried thyme

1 teaspoon dried basil

This sauce is rich, thick and a real crowd-pleaser. It takes a while to make, but it is so worth it. Make it the night before if you need to.

Place oil, onions, carrots, celery and zucchini in a large, deep saucepot over medium-heat. Cook, stirring frequently, until all water from the vegetables has evaporated. This may take about 20 minutes. Add garlic and stir another couple of minutes. Continue to cook and stir until vegetables begin to turn golden brown.

Add the ground beef, salt, and pepper and brown the beef. Cook about 20 minutes more, stirring occasionally. Add the tomato paste and cook the meat mixture for another 5 minutes. Add the red wine and cook about 2 minutes or until the wine is reduced by half. Add enough water to the saucepan to cover the meat mixture by about an inch. Add bay leaves, thyme and basil. Stir and mix well. Bring to a boil and then reduce the heat to low and simmer for at least 2 hours. As the sauce cooks, add 1–2 cups water about every 20 minutes or whenever the mixture seems too thick. You should do this at least twice. Don't add all the water in the beginning; it must be added gradually over the course of the cooking time. Remove bay leaves and serve over spaghetti squash or roasted green beans. Makes 6 servings.

Like all good bolognese sauces, this one freezes well!

Paleo Pizza, Frampton Style

"Crust"

1 pound lean ground beef or turkey (turkey may give you a drier "crust")
1 teaspoon sea salt
1 teaspoon pepper

Preheat the oven to 350 degrees F. Press raw meat into a 9×13 glass baking dish and sprinkle with salt and pepper. Bake about 10 minutes. Do not overcook. Remove from the oven and set aside.

Sauce

1 (28 ounce) can tomato puree
1 teaspoon dried oregano
1 teaspoon dried basil
1 tablespoon garlic powder

Mix tomatoes, oregano, basil and garlic powder in a bowl and set aside.

Toppings

½ pound ground sausage (hot or sweet)
Sweet onions, sliced thin, to taste
1 red bell pepper, thinly sliced
1 jar of artichoke hearts in olive oil, drained and diced

Brown the sausage and sweet onions in a skillet over medium heat until onions are soft and meat is cooked through. Set aside.

Top meat "crust" with tomato sauce. Add sausage, onions, peppers and artichoke hearts to pizza. Try to spread everything evenly.

Place back into oven for 5–10 minutes more. Cut in squares and serve. Makes 4 servings.

Personalize the pizza by adding your favorite Paleo-friendly toppings.

Beef Stew with Hearty Vegetables

1   cup almond flour

1   teaspoon sea salt

1   teaspoon pepper

2   tablespoons garlic powder

2-3 pounds stew beef, cut into 1½-inch pieces

2   tablespoons coconut oil

3   celery stalks, finely chopped

3   carrots, chopped into 1½-inch pieces

2   turnips, chopped into 1½-inch pieces

1   parsnip, chopped into 1½-inch pieces

3   onions, roughly chopped

3   garlic cloves, minced

Thyme, to taste

1   tablespoon dried oregano

4   cups beef broth

1   bay leaf

In a Ziploc bag, combine almond flour, salt, pepper and garlic powder. Place stew meat in bag and coat thoroughly.

Heat coconut oil in a skillet and brown the beef. You will have to do this in batches.

Add to crock-pot.

Add celery, carrots, turnips, parsnip, onions, garlic, thyme and oregano to crock-pot. Cover meat and vegetables with the beef broth. Add bay leaf, and cook on low for 6–7 hours. Makes 6 servings.

This stew freezes well.

Molasses-Marinated Flank Steak

1-2 pounds flank steak

Marinade

½   cup molasses

2   tablespoons red wine vinegar

1   teaspoon dried oregano

½   teaspoon pepper

1   teaspoon onion powder

1   tablespoon lemon juice

2   garlic cloves, minced

In a Ziploc bag, combine molasses, vinegar, oregano, pepper, onion powder, lemon juice and garlic. Add flank steak and marinate in the refrigerator for about 6–8 hours.

In a grill pan or on the grill over medium-high heat, grill the flank steak for about 4 minutes on each side. Do not overcook.

Let rest for 5–10 minutes before slicing. Slice meat thin and cut against the grain. Makes 4 servings.

The molasses makes this a savory-sweet main course.

Crock-Pot Brisket with Onions

3   onions, sliced

2   garlic cloves, minced

1   5-6 pound beef brisket, trimmed of excess fat

1   teaspoon sea salt

2   teaspoons pepper

2   cups chicken broth

2   bay leaves

Place the onions and garlic on the bottom of the crock-pot.

Season the brisket with salt and pepper and place on top of the onion mixture.

Add the broth and bay leaves. Cover and cook on high for about 6 hours or until fork-tender.

Transfer the brisket to a wooden carving board and slice it against the grain.

Serve with onion mixture and a little liquid from the crock-pot. Makes 6 servings.

Got leftovers? Make Brisket and Sweet Potato Soup (recipe, page 92).

"Piggies in a Blanket"
(otherwise known as Cabbage Rolls)

Sauce

1	(8 ounce) can tomato sauce
1	tablespoon tomato paste
½	cup chicken broth
1	tablespoon dried basil
1	teaspoon sea salt

Pepper, to taste

Cabbage Rolls

1	large head cabbage, core removed
1	pound ground beef
2	cups fresh spinach, chopped
1	onion, finely diced
3	garlic cloves, minced
½	tablespoon dried parsley
½	tablespoon dried basil
2	eggs, beaten
1	teaspoon paprika
1	teaspoon sea salt
1	teaspoon pepper

Preheat oven to 350 degrees F.

In a large bowl combine tomato sauce, tomato paste, broth, basil, salt and pepper and set aside.

Place the cabbage in a pot of boiling water and cook for 5–10 minutes or until tender. Drain, then set aside to cool. Once cool, separate out leaves. Try to get 10–15 leaves if possible.

Mix beef, spinach, onion, garlic, parsley, basil, eggs, paprika, salt and pepper in a large bowl. Lay the cabbage leaves out on a flat work surface. Place approximately ¼ cup of meat filling on the bottom edge (stem end) of each cabbage leaf. Fold in the two outside edges of the cabbage leaf and roll up to enclose the filling. Place each cabbage roll seam-side-down on a greased 9×13 baking dish. Cover the rolls with sauce. Bake for 30–40 minutes or until meat filling is thoroughly cooked. Serve immediately. Makes 4 servings.

When I was a child, my mother made "piggies in a blanket" frequently. She never referred to them as cabbage rolls; I don't think they would have been as well-received if she let us know the blanket was actually cabbage!

Beef Tenderloin with Horseradish and Roasted Garlic

1   3-pound beef tenderloin roast
1   whole garlic head
Olive oil
⅓   cup prepared horseradish
½   teaspoon sea salt
½   teaspoon dried basil
½   teaspoon dried thyme
½   teaspoon pepper

Preheat oven to 350 degrees F.

Remove white papery skin from garlic head (do not peel or separate the cloves). Coat liberally with olive oil and wrap in foil. Bake for 1 hour.

Cool 10 minutes. Separate cloves and squeeze to extract garlic pulp. Discard skins.

Mash garlic pulp, horseradish, salt, basil, thyme and pepper in a bowl with a fork until blended. Set aside.

Preheat oven to 400 degrees F.

Rub garlic mixture over roast, massaging it into the meat. Fold under 3 inches of small end and place tenderloin on a broiler pan coated with olive oil. Bake for 30 minutes or until thermometer registers 140 degrees (medium rare) or desired degree of doneness.

Remove from oven, cover loosely with foil and let rest for 10 minutes. Slice and serve. Makes 4 servings.

Another great dinner party dish!

Kicked-Up Ground Beef

2   pounds ground beef

2   tablespoons coconut oil or olive oil

2   red bell peppers, chopped

2   sweet or red onions, chopped

2   zucchini, shredded

3-4 tablespoons chili powder

1   teaspoon red pepper flakes

¼   cup beef broth, plus additional broth to keep vegetables from burning

Sea salt and pepper, to taste

Place oil, peppers, onions and zucchini into a Dutch oven. Cook, stirring frequently over medium heat about 15–20 minutes or until most of the liquid from the vegetables has evaporated and the vegetables turn golden brown. Add a little broth to keep vegetables from burning.

Add the ground beef to the Dutch oven and cook until browned.

Add chili powder, red pepper flakes, beef broth, salt and pepper to the mixture and simmer, stirring frequently, over low heat for 10–20 minutes longer until beef is thoroughly cooked. Makes 4 servings.

FRAMPTON FAMILY FAVORITE!

You can enjoy this dish as is or use as a "taco" filling. Sometimes we put it in lettuce boats or on top of chopped romaine hearts. It's great with some fresh slices of avocado too!

Meatballs with Marinara Sauce

Marinara Sauce

2	tablespoons olive oil
1	sweet onion, finely chopped
4	garlic cloves, minced
2	(28 ounce) cans of diced tomatoes with their juices
½	cup fresh basil leaves
1	tablespoon dried oregano or Italian seasoning
	Sea salt and pepper, to taste

Meatballs

½	onion
1	tablespoon dried basil
1	tablespoon dried parsley
4	garlic cloves
1	cup spinach
4	eggs, beaten
1	cup almond flour
2	teaspoons sea salt and pepper
2	tablespoons warm water
1	pound ground beef
1	pound ground pork
½	cup of the Marinara Sauce

Marinara Sauce:

Sauté olive oil, onion and garlic in a large saucepan over medium heat, stirring frequently, about 10 minutes or until onions have softened.

While onions are cooking, put tomatoes, basil, and oregano in a blender or food processor and pulse until smooth.

Once onion is softened, add tomato mixture to the saucepan. Bring to a boil over medium heat, then lower heat and simmer uncovered, stirring occasionally, for at least 1 hour. Sauce will reduce.

Meatballs:

Preheat oven to 350 degrees F.

Pulse onion, basil, parsley, garlic and spinach in a food processor. Remove and place in a bowl. Add eggs, almond flour, salt, pepper, water, beef, pork and ½ cup of the Marinara Sauce and mix well. Form golf ball-sized meatballs. Place in one or two large baking dishes in one layer and cook for about 15 minutes. Place meatballs in the sauce and simmer for at least 1 hour over very low heat. Makes 6 servings.

This dish freezes beautifully.

Spanish Beef

3   sweet potatoes

3   tablespoons olive oil

2   red or yellow bell peppers, chopped

2   sweet onions, chopped

2   pounds ground beef

½   tablespoon ground cumin

2   teaspoons ground coriander

1   tablespoon dried oregano

2   tablespoons paprika

1   teaspoon cayenne

1   bunch kale, chopped

1   cup pimento-stuffed green olives

Sea salt and black pepper, to taste

Coconut oil, if needed

Boil or bake the sweet potatoes until tender. Drain, cool and remove peel. Wrap in foil to keep warm.

While potatoes are cooking, heat olive oil in a large skillet over medium-high heat and add bell peppers and onions. Sauté about 15 minutes or until softened.

Add the ground beef and cook, stirring frequently, until all the beef has browned. Add cumin, coriander, oregano, paprika, cayenne, salt and pepper and mix well.

Add the kale and green olives. Continue cooking, stirring often until the kale is tender, about 5–10 minutes.

Meanwhile, mash the potatoes in a bowl with a fork or potato masher. Add a few teaspoons of coconut oil, if desired, and salt and pepper to taste. Serve beef over the sweet potatoes. Makes 4 servings.

Basic Paleo Meatloaf

1   sweet onion, diced
2   garlic cloves, minced
2   tablespoons dried basil
1   teaspoon dried marjoram
2   pounds ground beef
1   cup almond flour
4   eggs, beaten
3   tablespoons tomato paste
1   tablespoon Worcestershire sauce
1   teaspoon sea salt
2   tablespoons warm water
1   teaspoon pepper
1   (8-ounce) can tomato sauce, optional

Preheat oven to 350 degrees F.

Sauté the onion, garlic, basil and marjoram in a skillet with olive oil for about 10 minutes.

Mix remaining ingredients except tomato sauce in a large bowl. Add onion mixture. Mix well and pat mixture into a 8×5×2 inch loaf pan. Top with tomato sauce.

Bake for about 1 hour or until meat is no longer pink in the middle and a meat thermometer inserted into the thickest part reads 160 degrees F. Cover loosely with foil to keep warm and let stand at least 5 minutes before slicing. Makes 6 servings.

Meatloaf is one of my favorite comfort foods. I change up the basic recipe all the time to see what flavor combinations I can come up with.

BEEF

Amazing Beef Stew

4 pounds chuck beef, cut into 2-inch cubes

Sea salt and pepper, to taste

¼ cup coconut oil

5 onions, diced

3 carrots, diced

1 Anaheim pepper, seeded and minced

1 serrano pepper, seeded and minced

1 red bell pepper, minced

4 shallots, finely chopped

1 (6 ounce) can tomato paste

3 tablespoons paprika

1 teaspoon red chili flakes

1 teaspoon dried marjoram

1 teaspoon thyme

¼ cup balsamic vinegar

4 cups beef broth

2 bay leaves

Preheat oven to 325 degrees F.

Season the beef with salt and pepper.

In a large Dutch oven, over medium-high heat, add the coconut oil and heat for 1–2 minutes.

Cook the beef in batches, cooking each batch until browned before adding the next batch. Remove the meat from the Dutch oven and set aside.

Add the onions and carrots to the Dutch oven and cook uncovered for 15–20 minutes, stirring often.

Add the Anaheim, serrano, bell pepper and shallots. Cook uncovered, stirring frequently until vegetables have caramelized and all of the liquid has evaporated.

We love this over Mashed Sweet Potatoes (recipe, page 103)! Can't get enough of this stuff. Make extra to freeze.

Stir in the tomato paste and cook 1–2 minutes. Add in the paprika, red chili flakes, marjoram, and thyme. Mix well.

Deglaze the skillet with the balsamic vinegar and let reduce for about 2 minutes. Slowly add the beef broth. Add the beef and juices collected from the meat.

Add bay leaves. Season with salt and pepper, and stir gently to combine. Cover and cook in the preheated oven for 2–3 hours, stirring occasionally.

Remove the bay leaves and serve. Makes 6 servings.

Ultimate Chili

2-3 tablespoons olive oil

3 sweet onions, chopped

1 large zucchini, shredded

1 large summer squash, shredded

2 red peppers, finely chopped

1 jalapeño pepper, seeded and finely chopped

2 pounds ground beef

4 tablespoons chili powder

1 tablespoon cumin

2 tablespoons garlic powder

2 teaspoons dried oregano

2 tablespoons paprika

2 cups beef broth

1 (28 ounce) can diced tomatoes with their juices

Juice of 1 lime

Sea salt and pepper, to taste

Heat olive oil in large pot over medium heat. Add onions, zucchini, summer squash, red peppers and jalapeño pepper. Sauté for about 20 minutes until moisture has evaporated from vegetables, stirring frequently.

Add ground beef and cook until browned. Add chili powder, cumin, garlic powder, oregano and paprika and mix thoroughly. Add broth and tomatoes and mix well.

Simmer for about 30–60 minutes. Add the lime juice and stir. Add salt and pepper to taste. Makes 6 servings.

FRAMPTON FAMILY FAVORITE!

Freezes well.

Braised Short Ribs with Vegetables

12 beef short ribs, bone-in
2 tablespoons dried rosemary
Sea salt and pepper, to taste
¼ cup coconut oil
4 shallots, roughly chopped
3 medium carrots, peeled and cut into 1-inch pieces
2 sweet onions, roughly chopped
2 cups dry red wine
4 cups beef broth
2 tablespoons tomato paste

Preheat oven to 350 degrees F.

Season the ribs with rosemary, salt, and pepper.

Heat coconut oil in a large Dutch oven over medium-high heat. Once hot, add the short ribs and brown on each side for about 2 minutes. Remove the ribs and set aside.

Add the shallots, carrots, and onions to the Dutch oven. Cook for about 10 minutes, stirring frequently and making sure they start to brown. Deglaze the Dutch oven with the red wine and continue to cook over medium-high heat until the liquid is reduced to half (about 10–15 minutes). Add the beef broth and tomato paste and mix well.

Return the ribs to the Dutch oven. Cover and cook for 2–3 hours or until the meat is fork-tender and falling off the bone. Make sure to stir a few times during the cooking time.

Serve with the vegetables. Makes 4 servings.

Chinese Beef and Broccoli

6   cups broccoli florets

2   pounds sirloin strip steak, partially frozen and sliced thin

(partially freezing the meat helps make the slicing easier)

2   tablespoons coconut flour

1   tablespoon garlic powder

1   teaspoon onion powder

½   teaspoon cayenne pepper

3   tablespoons coconut oil or ghee (recipe, page 63), melted

2   garlic cloves, minced

2   shallots, minced

1   cup beef broth

¼   cup tamari

1   teaspoon arrowroot mixed with 2 tablespoons cold water

Steam broccoli florets in a steamer or in microwave and set aside.

Take sliced beef and place in a large Ziploc bag. Add coconut flour, garlic powder, onion powder and cayenne pepper. Seal bag and shake to completely cover all pieces of meat.

Heat coconut oil or ghee on medium-high heat in large, deep skillet and place pieces of the meat in the pan in batches. Cook for about a minute, flip and cook another minute. Remove to a plate. Continue until all meat is done.

Add minced garlic and shallots to the skillet and sauté for a few minutes. Pour broth into the skillet and scrape all the browned bits off the bottom of the skillet. Add tamari and bring to a rapid simmer. Add arrowroot mixture and stir thoroughly to thicken mixture. Add beef back to the skillet and mix to combine.

Remove from heat and spoon over steamed broccoli. Makes 6 servings.

When I crave Chinese take-out, this is the meal I prepare!

Chili Burgers

1 tablespoon olive oil

1 small onion, finely chopped

1 garlic clove, minced

1 jalapeño pepper, seeded and finely chopped

1 teaspoon cumin

1 pound ground beef

1 tablespoon chili powder

2 tablespoons fresh cilantro, leaves removed and finely chopped

½ teaspoon sea salt and pepper

Heat oil in a large skillet over medium heat. Add onions and sauté until soft and golden brown, about 5–10 minutes.

Add garlic, jalapeño and cumin and sauté another 5 minutes. Remove from heat. Let cool and place into a bowl.

Preheat grill to medium.

Add beef to onion mixture. Add chili powder, cilantro, salt and pepper. Mix well and form 4–6 patties.

Grill about 4–5 minutes per side and serve.

This can easily be turned into a chili meatloaf. Pat mixture into a 8×4×2-inch loaf pan and bake in a preheated 375 degree oven for about an hour or until a meat thermometer registers 160 degrees F.

Lamb

What's great about lamb is how it stands up to bold, vibrant flavors. Lamb pairs very well with the bright flavors of lemon, rosemary and mint. It's also great with garlic; garlic lovers can indulge and it doesn't overpower the meat but instead brings it to another level. Enjoy.

Moroccan Lamb Kabobs

¼ cup olive oil

2 tablespoons fresh cilantro, minced

2 tablespoons fresh parsley, minced

½ onion, grated

1 tablespoon paprika

2 garlic cloves, minced

1 teaspoon cumin

1 tablespoon fresh or 1 teaspoon dried rosemary

¼ cup lemon juice

1 teaspoon pepper

3 pounds boneless lamb roast, cut into 2- to 3-inch cubes

Mix all the ingredients (except lamb) in a Ziploc bag until well blended. Place lamb in the marinade and refrigerate at least 4 hours or overnight.

Preheat grill. Thread the meat on skewers and grill over medium-high heat for approximately 8–12 minutes, turning the kabobs every 4 minutes. Makes 4 servings.

Christine's Grilled Lamb Chops with Rosemary

6 lamb chops

Olive oil

Sea salt and pepper, to taste

1 tablespoon fresh or 1 teaspoon dried rosemary

Preheat the grill to medium.

Coat lamb with olive oil and then season with salt, pepper, and rosemary. Grill, turning at least once, 8–10 minutes or to desired degree of doneness. Serves 4–6.

Lemon Pepper Crusted Lamb Chops with Vegetables

1   tablespoon lemon pepper

2   teaspoons garlic salt or garlic powder

4   lamb loin chops

2   tablespoons olive oil

1   medium zucchini, halved lengthwise and chopped crosswise

1   bunch asparagus, ends trimmed, cut in half

10 Brussels sprouts, trimmed, cooked until crisp-tender and halved through the stem end

2   large tomatoes, roughly chopped

Juice from ½ lemon

Sea salt and pepper, to taste

Mix the garlic salt and lemon pepper in a small bowl. Coat the lamb evenly on all sides and set aside.

Preheat a large skillet over medium heat for 1 minute. Add 1 tablespoon of the olive oil and zucchini and sauté for 1 minute. Add the asparagus, Brussels sprouts and tomatoes and toss together. Add a pinch of salt and sauté for 5–6 minutes until tender, but not mushy.

Season with salt and pepper to taste and add the lemon juice.

While vegetables are cooking, preheat another skillet over medium-high heat for 1 minute. Add the remaining olive oil. Sear the lamb chops for 5 minutes each side.

Transfer chops to a plate, cover loosely with foil to keep warm and let rest for 5 minutes. Serve with the sautéed vegetables. Makes 4 servings.

Osso Bucco

¼ cup olive oil

4 lamb shanks (each about 1¼ pounds)

Sea salt, to taste

1 large sweet onion, roughly chopped

3 carrots, peeled and roughly chopped

3 celery stalks, roughly chopped

4 garlic cloves

1 (6 ounce) can tomato paste

2 cups dry red wine

1 tablespoon dried rosemary

1 tablespoon dried thyme

3-4 cups water

½ bag baby carrots

1 zucchini, trimmed and cut into 2-inch pieces

Preheat the oven to 350 degrees F.

Coat a large Dutch oven generously with olive oil and bring to a high heat.

Season the shanks with salt and add them to the Dutch oven. Brown well on all sides. Set aside.

Puree the onions, carrots, celery, and garlic in a food processor and process until the mixture becomes a coarse paste.

Add the pureed vegetables to the Dutch oven and season with salt. Cook the puree over medium heat until most of the water has evaporated and the mixture is beginning to brown, about 20 minutes, stirring frequently to prevent burning.

Add the tomato paste and continue to cook, stirring, for 5 minutes longer.

Osso Bucco is so amazingly tender; the lamb shanks almost melt in your mouth!

Stir in the wine, rosemary, and thyme. Stir frequently and cook until the wine has reduced by about half.

Add the shanks back to the pot and pour in 3 to 4 cups of water. Cover and cook in the oven for 2 hours, turning the shanks over about halfway through cooking time. Skim off the fat every 30–45 minutes.

Add the baby carrots and zucchini. Replace the lid and continue to cook 1 hour longer.

Remove the lid and cook, uncovered, 30 minutes longer to brown the shanks. Shanks are done when the meat is fork tender.

Transfer to serving plates. Serve with vegetables. Makes 6 servings.

Marinated Lamb Chops with Fresh Mint

3   pounds lamb chops
¼   cup olive oil
½   cup white balsamic vinegar
¼   cup dry white wine
3   garlic cloves, minced
½   teaspoon sea salt
½   teaspoon pepper
¼   cup fresh mint, chopped
1   teaspoon dried oregano
½   teaspoon red pepper flakes

Whisk together all of the ingredients (except the lamb chops) in a bowl and pour into a large Ziploc bag. Add the lamb chops to the bag and marinate in the refrigerator overnight.

Preheat the grill to medium.

Place chops on the grill and cook 3–4 minutes on each side.

Allow the chops to rest for 5 minutes before serving. Makes 4 servings.

My kids are not big fans of mint so I often omit it. Even without the mint, the chops taste great!

Lamb Meatballs with Eggplant and Tomato Sauce

Meatballs

1½ pounds ground lamb

½ tablespoon sea salt

1 tablespoon pepper

¼ teaspoon nutmeg

½ teaspoon cayenne pepper

½ cup fresh parsley, chopped

½ cup fresh mint, chopped

1 small onion, minced

3 garlic cloves, minced

1 tablespoon tomato paste

¼ cup pine nuts, ground in food processor

3 tablespoons warm water

½ cup olive oil (for cooking meatballs)

Sauce

3 medium eggplants

2 medium onions, finely chopped

3 garlic cloves, minced

2 (28 ounce) cans plum tomatoes

Sea salt and pepper, to taste

Meatballs:

Combine all ingredients except olive oil until well-mixed. With wet hands, form into golf ball-sized meatballs. Set aside.

Sauce:

Preheat the broiler and pierce the eggplants with a fork. Place them on a foil-lined baking sheet and broil in the top half of the oven until tender and the skin is charred, about 15 minutes, turning once. Remove eggplants from the oven. Using oven mitts, split each eggplant in half lengthwise to release the steam and some of the heat. Scoop out the eggplant flesh and drain it in a colander.

While the eggplant is draining, heat olive oil in a large Dutch oven and brown meatballs on all sides. You may have to do this in a couple of batches. Remove the meatballs and add the onions and garlic to the Dutch oven. Cook until soft and brown, about 10 minutes. Set meatballs aside. Stir in tomatoes and eggplant. Season with salt and pepper and cook for about 5 minutes.

Add the meatballs back to the pot. Partially cover and simmer for about 30 minutes. The eggplant and tomatoes should form a thick sauce. Makes 6 servings.

Desserts

Paleo desserts are definitely a contradiction of sorts. The dessert recipes are treats; that is how you need to think about them. They are not to be worked into your daily life. Treat yourself to these recipes once in a while; perhaps for a special day, holiday or dinner party. Remember, moderation is the key to healthy eating; Paleo or not!

Carrot Muffins

1¼ cups unsweetened coconut flakes
¾   cup blanched almond flour
1   teaspoon baking soda
½   teaspoon sea salt
1   heaping tablespoon cinnamon
1   cup baby carrots, grated
1   cup unsweetened applesauce
5   Medjool dates, pitted and chopped
4   tablespoons warm water
2   teaspoons vanilla extract
2   tablespoons coconut oil
3   eggs
¼   cup coarsely chopped pecans

There are many things you can do to change this recipe. Add a large pinch of ground ginger, nutmeg or cardamom; add ½ cup raisins or diced apples to the batter or substitute walnuts for pecans. (You can also add ½ cup chopped nuts to the batter.) The possibilities are endless!

Preheat oven to 350 degrees F.

Combine coconut flakes, almond flour, baking soda, salt and cinnamon in a medium-sized bowl. Set aside. In a separate bowl, mix together grated carrots and applesauce. Set aside.

In a medium microwave-safe glass bowl, add chopped dates and 3 tablespoons of warm water. Microwave for 30 seconds on high. Mash dates with a fork until they become paste-like. Add 1 more tablespoon of water, and microwave for another 30 seconds. Add coconut oil and vanilla to the date mixture and continue to mash until combined. The mixture will look oily. Mix the date mixture into the carrots and applesauce until combined. Slowly add the wet ingredients into the dry ingredients while you stir to mix. Make a well in the center of the batter. Beat the eggs with a fork and add eggs into the well. Blend the eggs into the batter until well-combined.

Use coconut oil to grease a standard-size muffin tin (2½ inches in diameter) or line the tins with cupcake liners. Divide the batter equally among the 12 muffin cups. Top with pecans and bake for 19–21 minutes or until a toothpick inserted in the center comes out clean. Cool the muffins in the pan on a cooling rack for 10 minutes. Makes 12 muffins.

Banana Bread FRAMPTON FAMILY FAVORITE!

½   cup coconut flour, sifted

¼   teaspoon baking soda

½   teaspoon sea salt

8   eggs

5   dates, chopped

½   tablespoon pure maple syrup

1   tablespoon vanilla

2   whole bananas, mashed

¼   cup coconut oil

¾   cup of "mix-ins" (raisins, chocolate chips, chopped pecans or walnuts)
or use ¼ cup of different "mix-ins;" one for each mini-loaf)

Preheat oven to 350 degrees F.

In a medium-sized bowl, combine flour, baking soda and salt. Set aside.

In a food processor, blend eggs, dates, maple syrup, vanilla and bananas.

Microwave coconut oil in a small glass measuring cup for about 30 seconds, or until melted. Cool slightly. Add coconut oil to the food processor and blend thoroughly.

Add wet ingredients to the dry ingredients and mix well.

Add raisins, chocolate chips, pecans or walnuts and stir to blend. Divide the batter into 3 greased mini loaf pans (8×4×2½ inches). Alternatively, you can make three different types of bread by adding a different mix-in to each batter-filled pan; use a spoon or small spatula to distribute the "mix-ins" evenly.

Bake in the center of the oven for 20–30 minutes or until a toothpick inserted in the center comes out clean. Do not overcook or the bread will be dry.

Let loaves cool on a cooling rack for 10 minutes. Cut into slices and serve warm or room temperature. Makes 3 mini loaves.

DESSERTS

Almond Macaroons
adapted from paleodiet.com

1	cup blanched almonds
½	teaspoon cinnamon
1	tablespoon grated lemon zest
2	egg whites
¼	cup raw honey
2	tablespoons lemon juice

Preheat oven to 250 degrees F.

Grind almonds coarsely in a food processor then transfer to a bowl. Add cinnamon and lemon zest and mix to combine.

In the a separate bowl, beat egg whites until very stiff. Fold in honey and mix until just combined.

Mix lemon juice into almond mixture and blend. Add to egg whites and honey mixture and fold to combine.

Use a tablespoon to drop the batter onto an ungreased cookie sheet, 2 inches apart. Bake for 30 minutes.

Remove from oven and let cookies cool on the baking sheet set on a cooling rack for 10 minutes. Makes about 6 macaroons.

Who doesn't love a chewy macaroon?

Paleo Fudge "Babies"

1⅓ cups pitted dates, chopped
1   cup walnuts
4   tablespoons unsweetened cocoa powder
1   teaspoon vanilla

Place all ingredients in a food processor and process for about 30–60 seconds or until mixture is smooth.

Transfer the mixture to a bowl then use your hands to form 1-inch balls. Place the balls (or "Babies") on a parchment lined baking sheet, chill until firm and serve cool or room temperature. Makes about 12–14 Fudge Babies.

Note: Try these other flavor variations:

- Mix shredded unsweetened coconut, chopped nuts or raisins to the bowl of date puree.

- After forming the balls, roll the "Babies" in unsweetened cocoa powder, finely crushed nuts or unsweetened coconut flakes

- Substitute other flavorings for the vanilla, but take care not to add too much! Mint extract and coconut extract are two of my favorites.

- Add 2 teaspoons (or to taste) of finely ground coffee before pureeing the mixture. The coffee adds a wonderful mocha flavor.

If you don't have enough dates on hand, try using pitted prunes.

Chocolate Coconut Bars

¾   cup pecans

6   pitted dates, roughly chopped

1   tablespoon unsweetened cocoa powder

2   tablespoons coconut butter or oil (If you can find the butter, it's better. Whole Foods carries it.)

2   tablespoons unsweetened shredded coconut

Put all ingredients in the food processor. Blend for 1 minute.

Shape into 1×2 inch bars and place on a parchment-lined baking sheet. Sprinkle with additional coconut flakes if desired. Chill, or enjoy at room temperature. Makes about 6 bars.

These sweet chewy bars are an addictive treat! I highly recommend you double this recipe; they will go fast!

Molasses Cookies

1½ cups blanched almond flour
¼   teaspoon sea salt
⅓   teaspoon baking soda
1   teaspoon ginger powder
1   heaping teaspoon cinnamon
¼   cup coconut oil, melted
¼   cup molasses

Combine almond flour, salt, baking soda, ginger and cinnamon in a large bowl. Set aside.

Whisk oil and molasses in a medium bowl. Pour wet ingredients into the dry ingredients and mix to blend. Cover and chill the dough for 1 hour.

Preheat oven to 350 degrees F.

Roll the dough into 1-inch balls. Place on cookie sheets, two inches apart.

Bake for 8 minutes; do not overcook.

Let cookies cool on the baking sheet set on a cooling rack for 10 minutes. Remove the cookies to a plate, platter or the cooling rack and cool completely. Makes about 12 cookies.

If you love molasses, you won't be able to resist these soft, moist treats!

Chocolate Chip Cookies

4	dates, pitted and chopped
1½	cups walnuts
½	cup pecans
1	teaspoon baking soda
⅛	teaspoon sea salt
2	tablespoons coconut oil
1	egg
1	teaspoon vanilla
¼	cup unsweetened shredded coconut
½	cup dark chocolate chips (73% cacao or higher)

There are lots of Paleo-friendly chocolate chip cookie recipes but we like our version the best!

Preheat oven to 350 degrees F.

Grind dates in a food processor until a paste forms, about 40 seconds. Add walnuts and pecans and blend until very finely chopped, about another 20–40 seconds. Add baking soda and salt and pulse a few more times.

Warm the coconut oil in a small microwave-proof bowl or a glass measuring cup in the microwave oven until melted. With the food processor running, drizzle oil into the batter, and add the egg and vanilla. Process until just combined; do not over-mix.

Scrape the batter into a large bowl and stir in coconut and chocolate chips with a wooden spoon. The dough will be sticky and wet. Drop 12 tablespoon-sized portions of the batter onto an ungreased cookie sheet and flatten slightly with your fingers.

Bake 10–15 minutes depending on your oven. Cookies will be slightly browned. Let cookies cool on the baking sheet set on a cooling rack for 10 minutes. Transfer the cookies to a plate, platter or the cooling rack to cool completely. Makes about 18 cookies.

FRAMPTON FAMILY FAVORITE!

Blueberry-Coconut Muffins

½ cup coconut oil, melted and cooled

8 eggs

½ cup unsweetened applesauce or 1 mashed small banana

½ teaspoon vanilla extract

½ cup coconut flour

¼ teaspoon baking soda

½ teaspoon cream of tarter

½ teaspoon sea salt

1 cup fresh or frozen blueberries

Preheat oven to 375 degrees F.

Blend together oil, eggs, applesauce or banana and vanilla in a large bowl.

Combine flour, baking soda, cream of tartar and salt in a separate large bowl. Add wet ingredients to dry ingredients and stir until mixture is smooth with no lumps.

Fold in blueberries. (Note: if using frozen blueberries, there's no need to thaw them.)

Grease a 12-cup muffin tin with coconut oil and fill each muffin tin about ¾ full.

Bake for about 18–20 minutes or until golden brown on top and a toothpick inserted in the center comes out clean. Cool muffins for 10 minutes in the tins. Makes 12 muffins.

FRAMPTON FAMILY FAVORITE!

Add walnuts for extra texture. So good!

Fresh Blueberry Cobbler

3-4 cups of fresh blueberries, rinsed

4   tablespoons raw honey

4   Breakfast Squares, crumbled (recipe page 27)

1   cup almond flour

2   teaspoons cinnamon

1   tablespoon coconut oil, melted

Cold coconut milk or almond milk, to taste

Preheat oven to 350 degrees F.

Pour the blueberries into a lightly greased 8×8 glass baking dish. Drizzle 2 tablespoons of the honey over the blueberries.

In a small bowl, mix together the crumbled Breakfast Squares, almond flour, cinnamon and coconut oil. Mix well. The mixture will be very thick with some lumps.

Use your hands to crumble the mixture on top of the blueberries, distributing it evenly. Bake 30–35 minutes or until golden brown on top.

Remove from oven and drizzle the remaining 2 tablespoons of honey over the topping. Serve warm or at room temperature in individual bowls with cold coconut or almond milk poured on top. Serves 4.

Chocolate-Coconut-Almond "Cups"
adapted from health-bent.com

2 cups dark chocolate chips (73% cacao or higher)

½ cup coconut oil, melted

2 tablespoons coconut crystals

¼ cup shredded, unsweetened coconut

2 teaspoons coconut extract

20 whole raw almonds, toasted and cooled

Place the chocolate chips in the top part of a double boiler. Bring the water to a simmer; the chocolate will melt in about 5–10 minutes.

While the chocolate is melting, line mini cupcake pans with paper liners. Drop 1 tablespoon of chocolate into each paper liner. Swirl the mixture with the back of the spoon, making sure that the chocolate covers the sides and the bottom of the liner. Refrigerate for 10 minutes or until the chocolate has hardened.

In the bowl of an electric mixer, combine the coconut oil, coconut crystals, shredded coconut and coconut extract. Beat about 2 minutes or until smooth.

Drop about 1 tablespoon of the coconut mixture into the hardened chocolate shells. Pat down the coconut mixture and refrigerate about 10 minutes or until hardened.

Top each "cup" with the remaining melted chocolate. Smooth the chocolate to make a smooth, level top. Place an almond on top and refrigerate about 30 minutes or until hardened. Serve chilled. Makes about 20 "cups."

FRAMPTON FAMILY FAVORITE!

Make almond butter "cups" by changing the filling to almond butter; just add a ½ cup of almond butter to 1 tablespoon honey, mix well and there's your filling!

DESSERTS

221

Mark Sisson's Grok Rocks

3   (4 ounce) dark chocolate bars, chopped
1   pound pitted prunes

Place the chocolate in the top part of a double boiler. Bring the water to a simmer; the chocolate will melt in about 5–10 minutes.

While the chocolate melts, cover a cookie sheet with wax paper.

Remove the chocolate from the heat, add the prunes to the chocolate mixture and stir gently until prunes are coated with chocolate.

Spoon the prunes onto a prepared baking sheet and place in the freezer for about 20 minutes until chilled. Makes about 20–25 "Rocks."

FRAMPTON FAMILY FAVORITE!

Chocolate-covered prunes? Yes! They're a big hit in my house; no matter how many I make, it's never enough.

Chocolate-Coconut Muffins

inspired by socialworkout.com

1   cup blanched almond flour

½   cup flaxseed meal

1   teaspoon baking powder

½   cup unsweetened cocoa powder

½   cup Ghiradelli unsweetened chocolate bar, finely chopped

1   cup shredded, unsweetened coconut

1   tablespoon brewed coffee, cooled

1   cup unsweetened applesauce

¼   cup maple syrup and 2 tablespoons

1   tablespoon distilled white vinegar

2   tablespoons coconut oil, melted

My sister, Nichole, made a wonderful birthday cake for me by pouring the batter into a greased 8×8 cake pan and baking. It was awesome!

Preheat oven to 350 degrees F.

Mix almond flour, flaxseed meal, baking powder, cocoa powder, chopped Ghiradelli chocolate and shredded coconut in a medium bowl.

In a separate medium-sized bowl, mix the coffee, apple sauce, all maple syrup, vinegar and coconut oil until blended.

Pour the wet ingredients into the dry ingredients and stir until blended. Pour the batter into 12 lightly-greased muffin tins (or, line the tins with paper cupcake liners).

Bake for 30 minutes; the muffins will be moist and a toothpick inserted in the center may be somewhat sticky. Do not overcook.

Remove the muffin tin from the oven and place a kitchen towel over the muffins. Let them "steam" for 10 minutes.

Serve warm with or without coconut milk ice cream. Makes about 12 muffins.

FRAMPTON FAMILY FAVORITE!

Apple Pie

Pie Crust

1   cup walnuts

1   cup almond flour

½   cup raw sunflower seeds

1½ cups pitted Medjool dates, chopped

Pie Filling

4   apples, peeled and sliced (if you like a tart pie, use Granny Smith
or Macintosh apples, but if you want a sweet pie use Pink Ladies or Cortland)

¼-½ cup lemon juice

½   cup water

2   tablespoons raw honey

1   heaping tablespoon cinnamon

Pinch of nutmeg

Pie Crust:

Preheat oven to 350 degrees F.

Combine all pie crust ingredients in a food processor and pulse a few
times to mix. Then process on high for about 45 seconds. The mixture
should be coarse and crumbly.

Place in an 8-inch pie plate, pressing dough to form a crust. Chill for
30 minutes.

Bake in the middle of the oven for about 20–30 minutes, checking
after 20 minutes to make sure it doesn't burn. Remove and allow crust
to cool while preparing the filling.

Sometimes before drizzling the syrupy liquid on top of the apples, I crumble Breakfast Squares (recipe, page 27) on top of the apples. The topping adds a nice texture to the pie.

Pie Filling:
Place all of the filling ingredients in a large saucepan on medium heat and simmer for 6–8 minutes, until apples are just tender.

Use a slotted spoon to transfer apples to a bowl. Allow the apples to cool for about 30 minutes.

Continue to cook the liquid in the saucepan until it thickens and then set aside.

Place apple filling into cooled pie crust and drizzle liquid on top.

Slice and serve. Makes 6 servings.

Pecan Cookies with Raisins and Coconut

1	cup blanched almond flour
1	cup pecans, finely ground
½	cup shredded coconut flakes
½	cup raisins
1	teaspoon cinnamon
6	tablespoons raw honey
¼	cup dark chocolate chips (73% cacao or higher)

Preheat oven to 350 degrees F.

Combine almond flour, pecans, coconut flakes, raisins and cinnamon in a large bowl and mix well.

Slowly add the honey while stirring constantly. The mixture will look a bit crumbly. Add the chocolate chips and mix to combine.

Use your hands to form balls with about 1½ tablespoons of dough. Place balls on a lightly greased cookie sheet about 2 inches apart. Use your hands to flatten each ball slightly.

Bake for 15–17 minutes or until light golden on top. Transfer the cookie sheet to a cooling rack and let the cookies cool for 10 minutes. Transfer cookies to cooling rack to cool completely. Makes about 1½ to 2 dozen cookies.

These are great even without the chocolate chips! The combination of raisins and honey make these cookies a sweet treat, indeed.

Pumpkin-Cranberry Muffins
adapted from gsscrossfit.com

1½   cups blanched almond flour

1   cup canned pumpkin puree

1   teaspoon baking powder

1   teaspoon baking soda

2   large eggs

⅓   cup maple syrup or raw honey

1½   teaspoons ground ginger

1   teaspoon vanilla extract

¼   teaspoon sea salt

½   cup dried cranberries

Preheat oven to 350 degrees F.

Mix together all the ingredients, except for the cranberries, in a large bowl until smooth. Fold in the cranberries and stir until just combined.

Spoon batter into 6 greased or paper-lined muffin cups, and bake for 20–25 minutes or until a toothpick inserted in the center comes out clean. Cool muffins for 10 minutes in the tins. Makes 6 muffins.

For variety, add ½ cup dark chocolate chips when you add the cranberries.

Paleo Chocolate Cupcakes

¼ cup coconut flour, sifted

¼ cup unsweetened cocoa powder, sifted

¼ teaspoon sea salt

½ teaspoon baking soda

¼ cup coconut oil, melted and cooled

½ cup raw honey

5 eggs

Preheat oven to 375 degrees F.

Combine flour, cocoa powder, salt and baking soda in a large bowl.

In a separate medium bowl combine coconut oil, honey and eggs and whisk to blend.

Add the wet ingredients to the dry ingredients and mix until combined.

Pour batter into paper-lined muffin tins, filling each cup about ⅔ full.

Bake for 18 minutes or until golden brown on top and a toothpick inserted in the center comes out clean.

Cool completely on a wire rack. Makes 10–12 cupcakes.

For a double-chocolate dessert, top cooled cupcakes with Paleo Chocolate Frosting (recipe, page 230).

Paleo Coconut Cupcakes

½   cup coconut flour, sifted

¼   cup coconut flakes

¼   teaspoon sea salt

½   teaspoon baking soda

⅓   cup coconut oil, melted and cooled

½   cup raw honey

8   eggs

2   teaspoons coconut extract

Preheat oven to 350 degrees F.

Combine flour, coconut flakes, salt and baking soda in a large bowl and set aside.

Mix coconut oil, honey, eggs and coconut extract in a medium bowl.

Add wet ingredients to dry ingredients and stir to blend.

Pour into 10–12 paper-lined muffin tins and fill each about ⅔ full with the batter.

Bake for 18 minutes or until a toothpick inserted in the center comes out clean. Cool on a wire rack. Makes 10–12 cupcakes.

These remarkably moist cupcakes are amazing! For a big splurge, serve them warm with coconut milk ice cream.

Paleo Chocolate Frosting

1   cup dark chocolate chips (73% cacao or higher)
½   cup coconut oil
2   tablespoons raw honey
1   tablespoon vanilla extract
½   teaspoon sea salt

Melt chocolate and coconut oil in a small saucepan over very low heat. Mix well to combine.

Stir in honey, vanilla and salt. Mix well.

Scrape mixture into a stainless steel bowl and place in the freezer for 10-20 minutes to chill.

Remove from freezer and whip frosting mixture with a hand blender until it is thick and fluffy.

Use the frosting for cupcakes (recipes, pages 228 and 229). Frosts approximately 12 cupcakes.

For a slightly sweeter chocolate frosting, use semi-sweet chocolate chips.

Dark Chocolate Brownies

2   heaping cups of walnuts or pecans

1   egg

½   cup agave

⅓   cup raw honey

1   tablespoon vanilla extract

½   cup unsweetened cocoa

½   teaspoon sea salt

1   teaspoon baking soda

2   ounces dark chocolate chips (73% cacao or higher)

Preheat oven to 325 degrees F.

Put nuts in food processor and pulse until the mixture is almost a crumbly paste, about 60 seconds. Remove nut mixture and place in a bowl. Set aside.

Whisk together egg, agave, honey and vanilla. Set aside.

Combine cocoa, salt and baking soda in bowl and mix well.

Blend wet and dry ingredients together. Add nut mixture.

Once blended smooth, add chocolate chips.

The batter will be extremely thick and sticky. Pour into greased 8×8 baking dish.

Bake for about 30–35 minutes.

Cool before cutting. Makes approximately 12 brownies.

Want to reduce the sugar? Substitute ½ cup unsweetened applesauce for the honey or agave.

Bibliography

Books:

- Wolf, R. 2010 *The Paleo Solution*, Victory Belt Publishing.

- Gedgaudas, N. 2009 *Primal Body–Primal Mind*, Primal Body-Primal Mind Publishing.

- Sisson, M. 2010 *The Primal Blueprint Cookbook*, Primal Nutrition, Inc. Publishing. *Recipes reprinted with permission: Primal Ketchup 51, BBQ Sauce and Grok Rocks.*

- Frangoso, S. 2011, *Everyday Paleo*, Victory Belt Publishing. *Inspired recipes: Apple Muffins, Butter Chicken, Spanish Beef, Warm Arugula Salad, and Apple-Shallot Pork Chops.*

Technical:

- Bohn, Torsten; Davidsson, Lena; Walczyk, Thomas; Hurrell, Richard Phytic Acid Added to White-Wheat Bread Inhibits Fractional Apparent Magnesium Absorption in Humans. *American Journal of Clinical Nutrition*. **2004**, 79, 418–23.

- Cordain, Loren; Eaton, S. Boyd; Sebastian, Anthony; Mann, Neil; Lindeberg, Staffan; Watkins, Bruce A.; O'Keefe, James H.; Brand-Miller, Janette; Origins and Evolution of the Western Diet: Health Implications for the 21st Century. *American Journal of Clinical Nutrition*. **2005**, 81, 341–54.

- Francis, George; Kerem, Zohar; Makkar, Harinder P.S.; Becker, Klaus; The Biological Action of Saponins in Animal Systems: A Review. *British Journal of Nutrition*. **2002**, 88, 587–605.

- Frassetto, LA.; Schloetter, M.; Mietus-Synder, M.; Morris, RC. Jr.; Sebastian, A.; Metabolic and Physiologic Improvements from Consuming a Paleolithic, Hunter-gatherer Type Diet. *EJCN*. **2009**, 0954–3007, 1–9.

- Jonsson, Tommy; Granfeldt, Yvonne; Ahren, Bo; Branell, Ulla-Darin; Palsson, Gunvor; Hansson, Anita; Soderstrom, Margareta; Lindeberg, Staffan; Beneficial Effects of a Paleolithic Diet on Cardiovascular Risk Factors in Type 2 Diabetes: A Randomized Cross-over Pilot Study. *Cardiovascular Diabetology*. **2009**, 8:35.

- Jonsson, Tommy; Granfeldt, Yvonne; Erlanson-Albertsson, Charlotte; Ahren, Bo; Lindeberg, Staffan; A Paleolithic Diet is More Satiating Per Calorie Than a Mediterranean-like Diet in Individuals with Ischemic Heart Disease. *Nutrition & Metabolism*. **2010**, 7:85.

- Konner, Melvin, MD, PhD.; Eaton, S. Boyd, MD. Paleolithic Nutrition Twenty-Five Years Later. *Nutrition in Clinical Practice*. **2010**, 25, 594–601.

- Lindeberg, S.; Jonsson, T.; Granfeldt, Y; Borgstrand, E.; Soffman, J.; Sjostrom, K.; Ahren, B.; A Paleolithic Diet Improves Glucose Tolerance more than a Mediterranean-like Diet in Individuals. *Diabetologia*. **2007**, 50, 1795–1807.

- Sjolander, Anita; Magnusson, Karl-Eric; Latkovic, Stevan; Morphological Changes of Rat Small Intestine After Short-Time Exposure to Concanavalin A or Wheat Germ Agglutinin. *Cell Structure and Function*. **1986**, 11, 285293.

- Vasconcelos, Ilka M.; Oliveria, Jose Tadeu A.; Antinutritional Properties of Plant Lectins. *Toxicon*. **2004**, 44, 385–403.

Websites for Consideration

- www.robbwolf.com
- www.thepaleodiet.com
- www.marksdailyapple.com
- www.everydaypaleo.com

Index

About the AUTHOR

Diane Frampton is a full-time working mother of two, committed to living a Paleo lifestyle. She is an avid CrossFitter at North Shore CrossFit, who is dedicated to educating herself about nutrition and the science of metabolism. She spends her free time creating healthy Paleo-friendly recipes to share.

Diane lives on the North Shore in Topsfield, Massachusetts with her husband and two daughters.